Bible Word Search

Delightful, Informative, and Entertaining Puzzles for All Ages

Ideal for Classroom Use

William C. Gordon

BAKER BOOK HOUSE

Grand Rapids, Michigan 49506

INSTRUCTIONS

No Bible dictionary is needed to work *Bible Word Search* puzzles—just a pen or pencil. Some of the words hidden in the alphabet diagram are easy to spot; others are elusive and require a bit of concentration. All words are always found in a straight line, either *forward, backward, up, down, or diagonally.* Some words overlap, so you will use some letters more than once. If you want a greater challenge, cover up the word list on the lefthand page. In some of the puzzles you are first asked to do some matching. Regardless of how well you scored on the matching exercise, you can go right on with your search for the words hidden in the alphabet diagram. When you find a word, cross it through on the word list opposite the puzzle and circle the word in the diagram. Have fun!

Copyright © 1974 by Baker Books
a division of Baker Book House Company
P.O. Box 6287, Grand Rapids, MI 49516-6287

Trade paperback issued 1983

ISBN: 0-8010-3679-8

Twelfth printing, February 1997

Printed in the United States of America

CONTENTS

1
CHRISTIAN VIRTUES

Hidden in this puzzle are twenty-four Christian virtues mentioned in the New Testament.

Contentment (Heb. 13:5)
Diligence (II Peter 1:10)
Faith (Mark 11:22)
Gentleness (II Tim. 2:24)
Godliness (II Peter 1:5-7)
Holiness (I Peter 1:15-16)
Honesty (Rom. 12:17)
Hospitality (Heb. 13:2)
Humility (I Peter 5:5)
Kindness (Eph. 4:32)
Liberality (Rom. 12:13)
Love (Matt. 5:44)
Meekness (Titus 3:2)
Obedience (Matt. 7:21)
Patience (Heb. 10:36)
Peaceableness (Heb. 12:14)
Prayerfulness (I Thess. 5:17)
Purity (Matt. 5:8)
Respect (Rom. 13:1-7)
Sympathy (Rom. 12:15)
Temperance (I Cor. 9:25)
Thankfulness (Eph. 5:20)
Truthfulness (Eph. 4:25)
Zeal (Titus 2:14)

1
CHRISTIAN VIRTUES

```
H O L I N E S S A O X B T C A S
O O U B Y H T A P M Y S O F S E
N A S V O A C Y B E H N S E C A
E S C P D N T V C A T S N N R H
S S H O I I B N D E E L E D E S
T E A V R T E X N N U G A C S B
Y N O U H I A T E F I S L E P P
T I P A D O M L H L S A N B E L
I L N E C E T T I E D L H A C O
L D B X N N U D N T U O C N T B
I O H T E R O L B F Y E H W O T
M G A G T B U A R T A C T P S E
U G H P I F X E I B H G E B S M
H E B O K L Y L L O V E P S E P
A C J N O A A E C K B X E I N E
G I A L R R N K D G J N T O K R
E H J P E E U H A E D U P H E A
T C E B S C P I G N W C K A E N
A H I S H E F A I T H P J G M C
P L A E Z B G K P A T I E N C E
```

2
NAMES FOR CHRISTIANS

In the New Testament Christians are given a variety of names. Twenty-three of these are hidden in this puzzle.

Athletes (II Tim. 2:5)

Believers (Acts 5:14)

Brethren (Acts 6:3)

Children (Rom. 8:16)

Christians (I Peter 4:16)

Disciples (Acts 9:36)

Examples (I Peter 2:21)

Friends (John 15:15)

Heirs (Titus 3:7)

Husbandmen (II Tim. 2:6)

Kings (Rev. 1:6)

Pilgrims (I Peter 2:11)

Priests (Rev. 1:6)

Saints (Acts 9:13)

Servants (Col. 3:24)

Soldiers (II Tim. 2:3)

Sons (John 1:12)

Sinners (I Tim. 1:15)

Sojourners (I Peter 1:17)

Strangers (I Peter 2:11)

Vessels (II Tim. 2:21)

Witnesses (Acts 1:8)

Workmen (II Tim. 2:15)

NAMES FOR CHRISTIANS

```
D H U S B A N D M E N A I H I S
E A O E C N E R H T E R B K D N
G N G S F E B N B Y Z O M N U A
S F B S G N I K E G I H E A F I
Z A D E H O W X L J K I X E J T
S A I N T S T S I N R R A O P S
B J V T I U E B E F C O M E E I
W Y C I O T A R V M L D P E D R
S O V W E S D V E S S E L S I H
E Q U L O L K A R K M P E S S C
R X H W I T I E S L R D S M C E
V T P H O J N O H I C I F I I B
A R C M L R L G E P N K H R P G
N S O N U D K S M N L I J G L H
T W E O I F T M E Q U A N L E O
S Z J E Y S X R E P T X R I S T
D O R B N V S O A N U O R P S S
S S C S R E G N A R T S Y V Z R
```

THE WORK OF THE HOLY SPIRIT

The Holy Spirit performs many functions. In the first group of sentences below are listed twelve activities of the Holy Spirit, as described in the Bible. The boldface verbs are hidden in this puzzle, as are the five boldface verbs from the second group of sentences, which describe the ways in which men work against the power of the Holy Spirit.

He **strives** with sinners (Gen. 6:3).

He **reproves** of sin (John 16:8).

He **helps** our infirmities (Rom. 8:26).

He **comforts** (Acts 9:31).

He **teaches** (John 14:26).

He **guides** (John 16:13).

He **sanctifies** (Rom. 15:16).

He **testifies** of Christ (John 15:26).

He **glorifies** Christ (John 16:14).

He **searches** all things (I Cor. 2:10).

He **works** according to His own will (Heb. 2:4).

He **dwells** in saints (John 14:17).

He may be **grieved** (Eph. 4:30).

He may be **vexed** (Isa. 63:10).

He can be **resisted** (Acts 7:51).

He can be **tempted** (Acts 5:9).

He can be **quenched** (I Thess. 5:19).

3
THE WORK OF THE HOLY SPIRIT

```
G D H I P O H S E I F I T S E T
L U E H O J I M K G O D L I I F
O P I V G S E H C A E T F U F V
R R I D E F R I E H T E Q M E N
I D S L E I K J C I D C O X E P
F O T P R S R N D S D R E Z C S
I M R R L N E G X E Y D A N S E
E L O A N U W Y T H T O L P T V
S I F B Q O C P E C H S L I R O
C W M M I A M O D R E E I P I R
B O O T S E S M T A H D B S V P
W V C U T R S L L E W D O Q E E
S A N C T I F I E S W O R K S R
```

4
DANIEL: THE BRAVE ONE

Daniel's bravery in the face of overwhelming odds proved his faith in God. God rewarded this faith by giving him positions of great authority. The boldface words in this biographical sketch are hidden in the puzzle. All of the Scripture references except the last one are from the Book of Daniel.

Daniel's name means **"God is my judge."**
Was captured when **Jehoiakim** was king of **Judah** (1:1).
Was taken from **Jerusalem** to Babylon (1:1-2).
With his three friends he **refused** to eat the king's food (1:8).
Was made to **study** for three years (1:5).
With his three friends he was found to be ten times **wiser** than the others (1:20).
Interpreted the king's **dream** of the great **image** (2:31-45).
Lived in the court of King **Nebuchadnezzar** (2:49).
His three friends were cast into a fiery **furnace** (3:16-23).
They were taken out **unharmed** (3:26-27).
Interpreted the king's dream of the great **tree** (4:20-27).
Read the **handwriting** on the wall for King **Belshazzar** (5:13-28).
Was made a **president** by King **Darius** (6:2).
A **trap** was laid for Daniel (6:6-9)
Continued to **pray** as before (6:10).
Was cast into the **den** of **lions** (6:16).
God **shut** the lions' **mouths** (6:22).
Daniel's **enemies** punished instead (6:24).
Had a **vision** of the four **beasts** (7:1-12).
Had a vision of a **ram** and a **goat** (8:1-14).
Had a vision of the **seventy weeks** (9:20-27).
Had a vision of the **last days** (chap. 10).
Jesus referred to the **prophecy** of Daniel (Matt. 24:15).

4
DANIEL: THE BRAVE ONE

```
H R A Z Z E N D A H C U B E N G
A P L A S T D A Y S N O S A P O
N P R A Y N C T V H P H W T X D
D A T O L V B K A I T A U L O I
W H B A P C X R L U N H R A N S
R E S I W H M A O F S L A T I M
I B W C O E E M H I U D E N V Y
T H A X D N B C T L O R C X B J
I W O M A E R D Y O P I N L T U
N C H I G C N L O R N C H A X D
G B E A S T S W E R A M O L C G
E O M H L D C T A L J G W N O E
S I K I N G E Z H N O I S I V T
E Y A N K D Z S C L B N U W D L
I T J U D A H G U D O H L E E O
M N H O H N I D N I T C S I V W
E E B S U B A O L N R U T R E E
N V L O H L N T H C F A U H N E
E E X T N E D I S E R P D I T K
B S M E L A S U R E J L Y N Y S
```

5
DREAMS AND DREAMERS

In Bible times God often sent messages to men in dreams. Match the dreams in the first column with the persons in the right column. Then find the name of the dreamer and the boldface words in the puzzle. Words may appear singly or in groups.

DREAM	Dreamer
1. _____ **Seven fat kine** and seven **thin kine**	A. Solomon
2. _____ **Ladder** that reached to heaven	B. Baker
3. _____ Great **image** with head of **gold** and feet of **clay**	C. Pharaoh
4. _____ **Sheaves** bowed down to him	D. Job
5. _____ Great **tree** that reached to **heaven**	E. Pilate's wife
6. _____ Given a **choice** of **riches, long life** or **wisdom**	F. Nebuchadnezzar
7. _____ Told to go to **Egypt**	G. Butler
8. _____ Told not to go back to **King Herod**	H. Nebuchadnezzar
9. _____ **Suffered** because of Jesus' **trial**	I. Jacob
10. _____ Had **baskets of grapes** on his head	J. Joseph, son of Jacob
11. _____ Had baskets of **bread** on his **head**	K. Joseph, husband of Mary
12. _____ **Frightened** by his dreams	L. Wise men

5
DREAMS AND DREAMERS

```
J O S E P H S O N O F J A C O B
O P B I D E E R T L A D D E R N
S H I R C T E I N C T C S A N E
E A C L S K R P O L H I U E T B
P R O N A C I B T A U O M K R U
H A S B U T Y R S Y N E I E S C
H O W L Q H E A D R S C A C D H
U H R I C H E S J I T D O W E A
S K C A T U H O W S K E S I R D
B V D E N E T H G I R F T S E N
A T G R A P E S N O F N E D F E
N U W V L O N G L I F E K O F Z
D N E V A E H D O H N C S M U Z
O S C P S E V E N I K T A F S A
F I T U K J Q U K O R O B L D R
M D A O C T L N C I M A G E T E
A X D U P B I C A U L O V I C L
R C O Y I H N L N I G O L D Z T
Y A G L T C O H J A D E J O B U
N E B U C H A D N E Z Z A R S B
```

6
THE HEBREW ALPHABET

Hidden in this puzzle are the names of the letters of the Hebrew alphabet. Hebrew was the original language of the Old Testament. Of interest is the fact that the sections of Psalm 119 are prefaced with letters of the Hebrew alphabet.

'aleph	teth	pe
beth	jodh	sadhe
gimel	kaph	qoph
daleth	lamedh	resh
he	mem	sin
waw	nun	shin
zayin	samekh	taw
heth	'ayin	

7
THE GREEK ALPHABET

Hidden in this puzzle are the names of the letters in the Greek alphabet. The New Testament originally was written in the Greek language.

alpha	iota	rho
beta	kappa	sigma
gamma	lambda	tau
delta	mu	upsilon
epsilon	nu	phi
zeta	xi	khi
eta	omicron	psi
theta	pi	omega

6
THE HEBREW ALPHABET

```
A B E W S H I N T L O Q A I P K
Z Y J A B E C N U N M O Z H A J
A U I W A T G T B A I P K P Q G
Y S I N Q H A L E P H H H G I F
I X R D D P Q M T R T K Y M L E
N W T E T H O E H N E X E K Z H
Y H M Q M P N U I T L L W M O D
P A S E N R E S H V A M C I A A
L T M R O Q P O N M D J O D H S
```

7
THE GREEK ALPHABET

```
O B U Z A I S P D I H G A M M A
A M D I S A D B M A L D E G L P
A B I R V R T D G A F U E P D P
T X O C Q E P E C T K T H L Q A
E N T A R O M U B E T A V W T K
H S A X B O A T C Z N S M P X A
T C J K U J N O L I S P U G E F
M O L H K N A H E Y H A L M I Y
E P S I L O N R Z G T P W P Z S
```

8
GOD IS...

The adjectives hidden in this puzzle describe the attributes of God as they are revealed in the Bible.

compassionate
eternal
faithful
glorious
good
holy
infinite
invisible
jealous
just
living
longsuffering
loving
majestic

merciful
omnipresent
omnipotent
omniscient
perfect
powerful
righteous
sovereign
supreme
true
upright
unchangeable
wise

8
GOD IS...

```
Y  L  O  H  X  G  L  U  F  I  C  R  E  M  F  E
A  Q  O  M  D  S  S  U  O  L  A  E  J  F  A  G
L  E  W  B  N  A  C  E  F  A  J  K  D  N  I  L
A  O  G  C  V  I  N  R  U  P  R  I  G  H  T  U
N  E  N  M  I  D  S  M  Q  T  I  E  U  O  H  F
R  L  I  G  U  S  U  C  C  P  L  I  C  H  F  R
E  O  V  L  S  H  O  E  I  B  P  E  S  T  U  E
T  V  I  H  B  U  F  V  A  E  T  B  E  R  L  W
E  I  L  T  K  R  F  E  E  I  N  L  Q  G  J  O
K  N  G  J  E  T  G  F  N  R  B  T  L  P  E  P
J  G  U  P  R  N  N  I  E  I  E  O  J  U  S  T
Z  U  I  Y  A  I  F  E  S  R  R  I  O  T  U  N
A  K  F  H  E  N  G  I  S  I  I  N  G  I  P  E
R  O  C  T  I  Z  V  H  O  E  L  N  M  N  R  T
C  N  I  R  B  N  H  U  T  G  R  A  G  Z  E  O
U  L  D  U  I  O  S  Y  L  E  D  P  X  O  M  P
M  A  J  E  S  T  I  C  U  T  O  X  I  P  E  I
E  S  A  U  V  W  V  T  W  R  O  U  O  N  Q  N
W  M  W  I  S  E  I  V  X  E  G  N  S  Y  M  M
F  E  T  A  N  O  I  S  S  A  P  M  O  C  K  O
```

OLD TESTAMENT NAMES THAT BEGIN WITH "A"

Some of the names used in Old Testament times sound strange to us today. Some of the names in this puzzle are well known to Bible readers; others are less familiar. All begin with the letter **A**.

Aaron	Absalom	Ahithophel
Abda	Achan	Amalek
Abednego	Adaiah	Amaziah
Abel	Adam	Amittai
Abiah	Adonijah	Ammon
Abiathar	Adriel	Amos
Abiel	Agag	Amoz
Abihu	Ahur	Amram
Abijah	Ahab	Anak
Abimelech	Aharah	Aram
Abinadab	Ahasuerus	Ariel
Abiram	Ahaz	Artaxerxes
Abishai	Ahaziah	Asa
Abner	Ahijah	Asher
Abraham	Ahimelech	Azariah

9
OLD TESTAMENT NAMES THAT BEGIN WITH "A"

```
A H A Z A H A B E L A N D A F B
B H E S A B G K E T O N O R A A
N D A N G D A I A M O Z A C G D
E B F S C K B O M L B P K A N A
R A H A U A D A B I H U G B D N
A B E D N E G O K E L A M A L I
C I U W O A R T A X E R X E S B
M R B A K C D U B L A N H A D A
O A A R H A M O S X W P A C B N
L M D A T I C K A D O N I J A H
A D A M U H J I A H S I B A V C
S A C T A L H A T D A C N G H E
B O H I W A B I H R H X A U A L
A Z A R I A H N A A C U O R R E
N D N B K A D H J A B R A H A M
A L A N A C T I B N R A K O H I
K M A R M A B I M E L E C H A H
A T I O I A D R I E L U H B F A
N E D B K C A M I T T A I S B K
L K A M A Z I A H A I Z A H A C
```

10
HOLY THINGS

The word **holy** in the Bible may indicate righteousness, but more often it carries the idea of separation from the common and profane. That which is holy is consecrated to God. Hidden in this puzzle is a list of holy persons and things mentioned in the Bible.

holy **ground** (Exod. 3:5)

holy **sabbath** (Exod. 16:23)

holy **nation** (Exod. 19:6)

holy **convocation** (Lev. 23:7)

holy **tithe** (Lev. 27:30)

holy **people** (Deut. 7:6)

holy **God** (Josh. 24:19)

holy **vessels** (I Kings 8:4)

holy **name** (Ps. 103:1)

holy **mount** (Isa. 27:13)

holy **flock** (Ezek. 36:38)

holy **covenant** (Dan. 11:28)

holy **angels** (Matt. 25:31)

holy **prophets** (Luke 1:70)

holy **child** (Acts 4:30)

holy **scriptures** (Rom. 1:2)

holy **lump** (Rom. 11:16)

holy **root** (Rom. 11:16)

holy **children** (I Cor. 7:14)

holy **temple** (Eph. 2:21)

holy **apostles** (Eph. 3:5)

holy **calling** (II Tim. 1:9)

holy **brethren** (Heb. 3:1)

holy **priesthood** (I Peter 2:5)

holy **men** (II Peter 1:21)

holy **conversation** (I Peter 1:15)

holy **faith** (Jude 20)

holy **city** (Rev. 21:2)

holy **Jerusalem** (Rev. 21:10)

10
HOLY THINGS

```
N O I T A C O V N O C F C F A C
H O A G J H G I P N O I T A N O
A K G R O U N D O D T E R I T V
I M N E M D I T T Y I G H T E E
P R O P H E T S U M A M E H M N
L A T U D L E M O S E D K O P A
I I S K N I B M C L C N L S L N
H T T N I T A F A I G H C I E T
N Q U O N I E S A N C R A T H E
O T J I O N U F I G I S T E L C
I S S L P R B L N P I O L S M N
T K V R E P L E T O R P A P A E
A C U J V A E U S W O Q M I H R
S O S V C L R P L E S U N T O D
R L L A E E P I P E L A I O X L
E F E S S A I N E R H T E R B I
V A S L E G N A B N I E S P Y H
N E S T S A B B A T H R U O A C
O N E S A I R I Z C E S R I P T
C O V T R D O O H T S E I R P A
```

ANOINTINGS

During Old Testament times when something was to be set aside for special use in the worship of God, it was often anointed with oil to show its special purpose. Persons who were to be God's special servants were also often anointed. Here is a list of things and persons that were anointed in this way. Can you find them in the puzzle?

THINGS

Altar (Exod. 29:36)
Ark (Exod. 30:26)
Tabernacle (Exod. 30:26)
Vessels (Num. 7:1)

PERSONS

Aaron (Exod. 28:41)
David (I Sam. 16:12-13)
Elisha (I Kings 19:16, 19)
Hazael (I Kings 19:15)
Jehoahaz (II Kings 23:30)
Jehoash (II Kings 11:12, 21)
Jehu (I Kings 19:16)
Saul (I Sam. 10:1)
Solomon (I Kings 1:34, 39)

11

ANOINTINGS

```
J  N  G  A  B  H  I  B  C  P  H  I  T
E  E  B  W  C  F  D  N  O  R  A  A  E
H  M  H  I  X  A  U  C  D  A  B  L  C
O  P  C  O  L  D  V  Z  G  E  C  T  B
A  E  M  X  A  B  F  J  R  O  F  A  X
S  G  S  V  G  H  T  N  V  P  L  R  G
H  N  I  O  C  J  A  C  T  A  H  L  K
A  D  V  H  F  C  C  Z  Y  W  I  R  D
X  S  A  U  L  A  B  D  A  C  S  H  J
L  B  D  E  G  V  S  K  R  E  O  P  V
A  W  H  O  L  N  A  Y  K  T  L  D  C
L  J  M  G  H  I  F  U  G  Y  O  A  J
V  E  S  S  E  L  S  N  R  K  M  J  Q
B  H  L  V  M  O  R  H  I  K  O  T  U
S  U  P  Z  T  J  B  U  A  V  N  H  I
R  I  G  D  A  L  E  Q  N  U  S  A  D
```

12
SAMSON: THE WEAK STRONG MAN

Samson is mentioned among many other heroes of faith in Hebrews 11. The boldface words in the following biographical sketch are hidden in the puzzle. All of the references are from the Book of Judges.

Son of **Manoah** (13:2).
Of the **tribe** of **Dan** (13:2).
His **birth** was foretold by an **angel** (13:3).
Was a **Nazarite** unto **God** (13:5).
Might **not** have his **hair** cut (13:5).
Married a **Philistine** wife (14:1-3).
Killed a **lion** with his bare hands (14:5-6).
Told a **riddle** to the Philistines (14:12-14).
Killed **thirty** Philistines (14:19).
His **wife** was given to another (14:20).
Caught three hundred **foxes** (15:4).
Destroyed the **crops** of the Philistines (15:5).
Slew a thousand Philistines with a **jawbone** (15:15).
Carried the **gates** of Gaza to the top of a **hill** (16:3).
Delilah tried to find the source of his strength (16:6).
Was **bound** with green **withs** (16:7).
Was bound with new **ropes** (16:11).
His hair was **woven** in a **web** and beam (16:13-15).
His hair was **cut** off (16:19).
The Philistines put out his **eyes** (16:21).
Was made to **grind** in the **prison** house (16:21).
Was brought to the Philistine **feast** (16:23-25).
Died when he pulled down the **pillars** (16:30).
Judged Israel for **twenty** years (16:31).

12
SAMSON: THE WEAK STRONG MAN

```
P  T  O  H  A  L  I  L  E  D  H  U  C
E  H  A  I  R  H  D  L  P  W  A  S  U
M  I  I  O  I  N  D  S  I  C  M  P  T
S  R  U  L  U  D  A  T  L  L  I  O  N
I  T  L  O  I  E  H  F  L  E  T  R  N
E  Y  B  R  O  S  R  E  A  G  F  C  O
Y  T  R  I  B  E  T  H  R  N  M  E  T
E  N  A  G  S  I  N  I  S  A  O  S  D
S  E  P  O  R  G  O  D  N  L  A  E  E
T  W  I  A  X  D  T  O  K  E  I  H  N
R  T  Z  P  O  S  A  N  F  R  F  R  O
E  A  L  D  D  H  O  N  R  O  H  I  B
N  A  T  N  K  S  C  A  X  D  B  E  W
G  J  H  I  I  K  M  E  U  L  N  D  A
T  B  I  R  T  H  S  E  T  A  G  P  J
H  O  P  G  A  L  R  S  N  E  V  O  W
```

13
"LORD, LORD"

The following inscription is found in Lubeck Cathedral and is based on Luke 6:46: "And why call ye me, Lord, Lord, and do not the things which I say?" The boldface words are hidden in the puzzle.

Ye call me **Master** . . . and **obey** me not.
Ye call me **Light** . . . and **see** me not.
Ye call me **Way** . . . and **walk** me not.
Ye call me **Life** . . . and **desire** me not.
Ye call me **Wise** . . . and **follow** me not.
Ye call me **Rich** . . . and **ask** me not.
Ye call me **Eternal** . . . and **seek** me not.
Ye call me **Gracious** . . . and **trust** me not.
Ye call me **Noble** . . . and **serve** me not.
Ye call me **Mighty** . . . and **honor** me not.
Ye call me **Just** . . . and **fear** me not.
If I **condemn** you . . . **blame** me not.

13
"LORD, LORD"

```
R  O  N  O  H  L  M  E  L  B  O  N  E  E  S  L
A  B  V  E  X  R  D  Z  K  U  M  G  V  A  I  U
Y  E  N  L  A  N  R  E  T  E  I  P  A  G  U  W
K  Y  G  E  T  U  E  Z  D  O  G  I  H  H  T  X
E  R  F  R  M  S  Y  N  E  O  H  T  S  F  R  Y
K  F  J  C  A  N  O  F  S  A  T  E  G  T  U  A
L  B  I  O  S  C  M  L  I  E  Y  B  M  R  S  W
A  E  P  L  T  A  I  X  R  K  S  C  E  A  T  J
W  I  Q  D  E  H  E  O  E  N  S  I  Q  S  L  V
O  H  C  I  R  S  W  A  U  O  E  O  W  K  I  B
T  S  U  J  I  E  V  R  E  S  F  O  L  L  O  W
```

FORTY OLD TESTAMENT PERSONALITIES

Here is a list of the names of forty people chosen from the Bible stories of the Old Testament. Most are well known. All of the names are hidden in this puzzle.

Aaron	Haman
Abel	Hezekiah
Abram	Jacob
Adam	Jehu
Amos	Jeremiah
Barak	Job
Benjamin	Joel
Boaz	Jonah
Cain	Judah
Caleb	Laban
Dan	Lot
Daniel	Mordecai
David	Noah
Eli	Obed
Esau	Reuben
Ezekiel	Samuel
Ezra	Saul
Gad	Shem
Gideon	Solomon
Ham	Zephaniah

14
FORTY OLD TESTAMENT PERSONALITIES

```
B  L  C  E  S  A  U  N  I  A  C  D  A  N  L  W
P  N  E  X  O  U  I  M  V  Q  E  Y  O  B  E  D
A  C  P  B  M  M  O  C  B  M  L  R  H  A  O  N
K  I  O  E  A  R  D  U  O  W  A  L  C  B  J  A
A  P  Z  J  R  A  A  R  Q  A  X  R  D  O  M  X
R  R  N  B  E  G  D  H  E  P  I  Q  B  V  H  E
A  E  D  F  H  E  S  A  M  U  E  L  U  A  D  C
B  E  L  A  C  G  C  L  M  E  K  P  I  O  M  T
O  C  H  A  J  B  L  F  R  B  S  M  T  C  I  O
A  H  I  L  E  K  H  C  L  O  E  N  A  B  A  L
Z  E  P  H  A  N  I  A  H  R  H  N  D  Q  E  U
G  Z  F  K  E  M  G  P  E  M  D  A  V  I  D  A
R  E  U  B  E  N  O  J  W  D  G  M  N  C  H  S
B  K  J  B  H  L  E  O  A  P  T  A  I  S  D  O
D  I  U  J  M  H  V  G  W  C  D  H  A  M  F  L
F  A  E  P  U  Y  I  M  B  N  O  X  E  O  L  O
S  H  E  M  B  D  E  C  I  R  U  B  J  B  I  M
B  J  F  K  E  O  A  H  A  N  O  J  G  V  C  O
G  H  C  O  K  G  L  H  F  P  B  W  E  K  B  N
D  L  N  F  M  B  T  Q  J  E  Z  E  K  I  E  L
```

AMOS: SHEPHERD FROM TEKOA

The prophet Amos was a shepherd and dresser of sycomore trees. His agrarian background is reflected in the book that bears his name. Hidden in this puzzle are forty-three words selected from the Book of Amos, all of which speak of agriculture and the countryside.

grass

corn

grain

wheat

grapes

summer fruit

olive

oak

sycomore

fig

hemlock

cedar

harvest

sheaves

threshing

king's mowings

latter growth

lion

bear

serpent

gardens

vineyards

mildew

palmer worm

wormwood

grasshopper

herdman

shepherd

plowman

reaper

husbandman

treader [of grapes]

horses

oxen

lambs

cows

kine

calves

flock

stall

bird

bow

snare

AMOS: SHEPHERD FROM TEKOA

```
K I N E B B E S D R A Y E N I V
A I B S I E V T R E A D E R H M
P O N G R A I N S S A R G E N S
W O H G D R L L A T S U M K H L
G R A S S H O P P E R L C E K S
D N R M W M C H V B O O P I N D
T M V I O U O L A C L H H A J P
H N E L C R A W K F E U R I V L
R A S D S C T G I R G E H K A O
E M T E O N A M D N A B S U H W
S D S W L R S W O M G G X W Y M
H R Z E D K O F R E I S I V S A
I E R E F R J O Y F X W B G E N
N H N Q M I W N W H E A T M P A
G S O W E R O M O C Y S N E A B
A B O C E I C R A D E C E F R L
T O O M L A R E P A E R X U G Z
D R L D L A T T E R G R O W T H
N A S H E A V E S E R P E N T C
P S O R P T I U R F R E M M U S
```

16
MOSES: THE LEADER

The writer to the Hebrews described Moses as a man who saw "him who is invisible" (Christ), and that this fact made him choose to suffer with the people of God rather than to enjoy the good earthly life that was offered to him. The bold-face words in the biographical sketch that follows are hidden in the puzzle.

Was a **beautiful** baby (Acts 7:20).

Belonged to the **tribe** of **Levi** (Exod. 2:1).

Was hidden by his mother in an ark of **bulrushes** (Exod. 2:3).

Was watched over by his sister **Miriam** (Exod. 2:4, 7; 15:20).

Was found by **Pharaoh's** daughter (Exod. 2:5-10).

Was given highest **learning** of the Egyptians (Heb. 3:2-3).

Chose to be with his own **people** (Heb. 11:23-26).

Killed an **Egyptian** who was smiting a **Hebrew** (Exod. 2:11-12).

Fled to the land of **Midian** (Exod. 2:15).

Kept sheep for his father-in-law **Jethro** (Exod. 3:1).

Was called by God through a **burning bush** (Exod. 3:2-5).

Asked **Pharaoh** to let the people of **Israel** go (Exod. 5:1).

Was helped by his brother **Aaron** (Exod. 4:27-30).

As God's servant, Moses brought the **ten plagues** on **Egypt** (Exod. 7 — 12).

Led the children of Israel through the **Red Sea** (Exod. 14:15-31).

Was fed **manna** (Exod. 16:14-15).

Struck the **rock** to get **water** (Num. 30:10).

Received the **law** of God on **Mt. Sinai** (Exod. 19:1-3).

Threw down and broke the first **set** of **tables** on which the commandments were written (Exod. 32:19).

Destroyed the golden **calf** (Exod. 32:20-29).

His **face** shown with the **glory** of God when he came down from the mountain (Exod. 34:29-33).

Built the **tabernacle** according to God's directions (Exod. 40:1-38).

Could not enter the promised land but **saw** it from **Mt. Nebo** (Deut. 34:1-4).

Was **buried** by God (Deut. 34:5-6).

Met with **Jesus** and **Elijah** on the Mt. of **Transfiguration** (Matt. 17:1-3).

MOSES: THE LEADER

```
L  B  E  L  O  M  T  S  I  N  A  I  M  D  E  B
A  I  T  N  I  S  V  E  R  G  S  T  G  O  Y  U
W  N  O  R  A  A  T  Y  N  H  N  U  K  S  N  L
D  S  I  H  N  G  R  I  O  E  O  T  C  U  H  R
O  A  N  F  T  O  N  A  B  J  X  N  O  S  E  U
M  E  U  V  L  R  R  O  N  H  E  B  R  E  W  S
A  L  I  G  A  A  N  A  C  L  S  T  S  J  L  H
N  C  P  E  H  R  C  K  P  K  P  E  H  E  U  E
N  A  L  P  G  T  C  O  S  H  U  P  A  R  P  S
A  N  O  W  A  U  E  N  W  G  C  R  H  U  O  A
A  R  V  C  R  P  G  R  A  T  S  A  C  M  H  U
W  E  L  T  O  H  Y  L  N  I  J  E  I  V  E  L
K  B  S  H  I  S  P  V  U  I  C  D  L  N  O  U
E  A  I  D  W  N  T  H  L  W  I  H  D  B  K  F
B  T  R  L  E  D  I  E  O  A  G  E  T  H  A  I
I  O  E  T  N  R  A  W  N  E  I  P  O  C  R  T
R  F  T  O  G  D  N  S  O  R  S  L  E  V  E  U
T  R  A  N  S  F  I  G  U  R  A  T  I  O  N  A
D  F  W  T  E  W  O  B  P  L  W  D  H  G  T  E
E  G  Y  P  T  H  S  U  B  G  N  I  N  R  U  B
```

17
"FEAR NOT"

Hidden in this puzzle are the names of individuals to whom God said, "Fear not." Sometimes the reassurance was given in a vision; other times the message was delivered by an angel; in a few instances Christ Himself gave such reassurance.

Abram (Gen. 15:1)
Daniel (Dan. 10:12)
Ezekiel (Ezek. 3:9)
Gideon (Judg. 6:23)
Hagar (Gen. 21:17)
Isaac (Gen. 26:24)
Jacob (Gen. 46:3)
Jairus (Luke 8:50)
Jeremiah (Lam. 3:57)
John (Rev. 1:17)
Joshua (Josh. 8:1)
Mary (mother of Jesus) (Luke 1:30)
Mary (wife of Cleophas) (Matt. 28:5)
Mary Magdalene (Matt. 28:5)
Moses (Num. 21:34)
Paul (Acts 27:24)

Simon (Luke 5:10)
Zacharias (Luke 1:13)
Zerubbabel (Hag. 2:5)

17
"FEAR NOT"

```
A N O M I S O A P G I D E O N
B Q R R U L I P U N O N I C B
I S A A C J E Q A H E U M O N
Y O G P T D H B G L S E S O M
F S A I R A H C A Z V O K L A
S A H E H Z I D Z B T B J V L
M S O R A H G A P S B S Z E E
D A C D I A I Y A S I U I U I
R P R E M C K G U A J N R I K
F B G Y E I U R L N A Y Z E E
A O R E R X I W I D C M R C Z
N A H F E A V L W T O X L A E
M N H O J M S M A R B A D A M
```

CITIES AND SITES (1)

First test your knowledge of the geography and history of the Bible by matching the city or site with facts in the first column. Then go on to find the names hidden in the puzzle.

1. _____ City, in the vicinity of which Joseph was sold into slavery
2. _____ Oasis where Israel encamped on its way to Canaan
3. _____ Trading center where Terah and Abraham stopped for a time
4. _____ Town where Jonathan defeated the Philistines
5. _____ Sumerian city; the home of Abraham
6. _____ Town where the ark remained for twenty years
7. _____ City of the plain to which Lot fled
8. _____ Town, near which was the cave which David used as a place of refuge
9. _____ Philistine city, the doors of which Samson carried off
10. _____ Town which served as a spiritual center for Israel before that of Jerusalem
11. _____ Home of Amos
12. _____ City where men thought Paul was a God
13. _____ Capital of Northern Kingdom in days of Jeroboam I
14. _____ Early home of Saul
15. _____ Place ruled by seventy-seven elders who refused to render Gideon assistance
16. _____ Town where David cut off the skirt of Saul's robe
17. _____ City where believers were first called Christians
18. _____ City whose walls fell down
19. _____ Town where Jesus restored to life widow's only son
20. _____ Place on Jordan's east bank where John baptized
21. _____ Region where relatives of the Biblical Patriarchs settled; home of Laban
22. _____ City of Macedonia where Paul made converts, including his jailor
23. _____ Seaport visited by Paul on 1st missionary journey
24. _____ Place at which Isaac dug a well

A. Adullam
B. Antioch
C. Bethabara
D. Dothan
E. Elim
F. En-gedi
G. Gaza
H. Gibeah
I. Haran
J. Jericho
K. Kirjath-jearim
L. Lystra
M. Michmash
N. Nain
O. Padan-aram
P. Philippi
Q. Rehoboth
R. Salamis
S. Shiloh
T. Succoth
U. Tekoa
V. Tirzah
W. Ur
X. Zoar

18
CITIES AND SITES (1)

```
G  S  I  M  A  L  A  S  A  G  T  E  K  O  A  H
I  C  K  O  P  R  S  H  M  L  N  M  B  N  U  C
B  D  B  R  T  A  F  A  I  T  T  A  E  K  D  O
E  B  L  S  J  I  D  R  A  O  I  K  I  Y  L  I
A  N  Y  J  C  U  Q  A  B  A  M  R  A  N  C  T
H  L  E  J  L  F  Z  N  N  C  J  W  Z  E  K  N
I  A  M  L  I  A  R  E  P  A  Q  B  P  A  V  A
A  M  A  Z  G  L  M  A  T  A  R  O  J  D  H  S
R  M  H  T  F  O  V  H  O  C  E  A  D  S  U  T
A  I  Z  S  U  T  J  I  S  Z  R  N  M  C  O  I
B  E  S  G  H  E  L  E  D  A  A  J  C  P  N  P
A  T  Y  G  A  I  O  K  R  H  M  O  Y  A  B  P
H  M  X  R  F  U  L  H  T  I  T  H  R  N  O  I
T  W  I  E  U  V  R  O  V  H  C  A  C  W  Z  L
E  M  H  L  J  G  D  C  H  U  H  H  W  I  Y  I
B  J  X  I  E  S  D  P  O  N  O  Q  O  X  M  H
R  E  H  O  B  O  T  H  D  I  D  E  G  N  E  P
```

CITIES AND SITES (2)

First test your knowledge of the geography and history of the Bible. Then start your hunt for the names given in the second column.

1. _____ Boyhood home of Jesus
2. _____ City of which Melchizedek was king
3. _____ Seaport to which Paul summoned the elders of Ephesus to exhort them and say farewell
4. _____ City of Asia Minor in which a Christian church was established, one that was poor but spiritually rich
5. _____ Seaport city in which Paul had his vision of a man in Macedonia
6. _____ The city which fell to Joshua following the victory at Jericho
7. _____ City where Hebrews settled during time of Joseph
8. _____ Birthplace of Samson
9. _____ Town near Jacob's well
10. _____ Where Jacob encountered God
11. _____ 1 of 5 leading Philistine cities
12. _____ City mentioned in the account of the healing of the demoniac
13. _____ Town where the parents of Samuel lived
14. _____ A desert place where bitter water was made sweet
15. _____ Town near where Abraham purchased a burial plot
16. _____ City occupied by the Jebusites until David's time
17. _____ City beseiged by Sennacherib
18. _____ The last stopping place of the Israelites on their journey to Canaan, before Sinai
19. _____ Village in which Jesus appeared to two of his followers after His resurrection
20. _____ City where Christ was born
21. _____ City where Jesus performed many miracles
22. _____ Greek city where Jews had a synagogue, in which Paul preached
23. _____ Town to which Elijah went after the brook Cherith dried up
24. _____ Town where a worship center was set up to counteract that of Jerusalem

A. Ai
B. Ashdod
C. Bethel
D. Bethlehem
E. Capernaum
F. Emmaus
G. Gadara
H. Goshen
I. Hebron
J. Jerusalem
K. Libnah
L. Marah
M. Miletus
N. Nazareth
O. Peniel
P. Ramah
Q. Rephidim
R. Salem
S. Smyrna
T. Sychar
U. Thessalonica
V. Troas
W. Zarephath
X. Zorah

19
CITIES AND SITES (2)

```
M I D I H P E R A M V I D A Y G
O W I B S S N M W L X U J N W A
A W R A Z A R E P H A T H R A D
H J O C I H O L A P V T M Y O A
N R E G Q R G A D H E W K M P R
T J V R Z P Q S F R N N E S V A
K K A E U G R S A T U V I R B O
F I M C D S O Z T Y D M U E T D
M H K J I F A L Q S E O U S L C
E M O L P N C L K H J E D A R E
L G I B U E O Y E B T M A H A M
H E F L O I R L P M H U D A S M
A S H Z E Z H H A G F A C Z A A
O N A T D T O D X S V N N E B U
D O N C E M U G J B S R U B Y S
M R L B Z B N S X S C E Y T I P
A B A G O S H E N A Z P H X D L
R E S O R L N F E R W A E T M O
I H A R A M A H R A H C Y S M I
D H S A H I R O X Z T K B O A C
```

CITIES AND SITES (3)

Here's an opportunity to test your knowledge of the geography and history of the Bible before you begin your search for the names listed in the second column.

1. _____ City associated with Sodom
2. _____ Philistine town taken by David and later ruled by the kings of Judah
3. Island visited by a ship on which Paul was a passenger
4. _____ City to which Jonah preached
5. _____ Home of Goliath
6. _____ City where Paul preached on Mars Hill
7. _____ Town through which the Israelites passed on their journey to Cannaan
8. _____ Town near which Naboth had his vineyard
9. _____ Town thought to be the home of the prophet Micah
10. _____ Hivite city that made an alliance with Joshua
11. _____ City where Philistines fastened the bodies of Saul and his two sons to a wall
12. _____ Birthplace of Jeremiah
13. _____ Phoenician city over which King Hiram ruled
14. _____ City famous for schools; most famous son, Paul
15. _____ Town in which Joseph's body was buried
16. _____ City Solomon strengthened; Josiah was slain here
17. _____ City whose name has become synonymous with a sexual aberration
18. _____ Town occupied by Philistines during Samson's time
19. _____ A city of refuge; home of Jephthah; site where Ahab was killed
20. _____ City in Asia Minor which receives only commendation in the Book of Revelation
21. _____ City where Saul began his military career
22. _____ City in Asia Minor where there existed a "lukewarm" Christian church
23. _____ Village in which Mary, Martha, and Lazarus lived
24. _____ City where Demetrius lived

A. Anathoth
B. Athens
C. Bethany
D. Bethshan
E. Elath
F. Ephesus
G. Gath
H. Gibeon
I. Gomorrah
J. Jabesh-gilead
K. Jezreel
L. Laodicea
M. Megiddo
N. Moresheth-gath
O. Nineveh
P. Philadelphia
Q. Ramoth-gilead
R. Rhodes
S. Shechem
T. Sodom
U. Tarsus
V. Timnah
W. Tyre
X. Ziklag

```
A R V O M E G I D D O P R L O J
S P H I L A D E L P H I A M A A
O E U U Z S D O I A H O D B A Z
J F O T E E L A O D I C E A T B
W I Z D R X R D I T E S A S H O
O N O N Z C I Y S C H H O R E T
F H V M Z I T D T G D Q T K N H
R I E L E A K B I S G R R A S H
H I H A R S M L I Q U A H S G T
E L Y S N L E Q A C T S B A C A
V G U I E A S L T G H J E Z E G
E S H K D X T U A T B M A H A H
N H H I N K V H E T G T O W P T
I A M G O J H B O O H A Y D V E
N N E G E F W F M T H K I Z O H
H M H J B O W O D A H A E B H S
S I C K I G R E L E E R Z E J E
H T E T G R C E O X B I D F T R
U O H D A E L I G H T O M A R O
M P S H R N B E T H A N Y P Q M
```

SYMBOLS OF CHRIST

Hidden in this puzzle are forty symbols of Christ. They range from animals, plants, and celestial objects to man-made objects.

Alpha (Rev. 1:8)
Anchor (Heb. 6:19)
Balm (Jer. 8:22)
Branch (Isa. 4:2)
Bread (John 6:51)
Cornerstone (Eph. 2:20)
Day Star (II Peter 1:19)
Dew (Hos. 14:5)
Door (John 10:9)
Ensign (Isa. 11:10)
Firstfruits (I Cor. 15:20)
Foundation (Isa. 28:16)
Fountain (Jer. 2:13)
Fruit (Isa. 4:2)
Horn (Luke 1:69)
Lamb (John 1:29)
Light (John 9:5)
Lily (Hos. 14:5)
Lion (Rev. 5:5)
Morning Star (Rev. 22:16)
Omega (Rev. 1:8)
Plant (Isa. 53:2)

Ransom (Matt. 20:28)
Rock (I Peter 2:8)
Rod (Isa. 11:1)
Root (Isa. 53:2)
Sanctuary (Isa. 8:14)
Seed (Gen. 3:15)
Sceptre (Num. 24:17)
Shadow (Isa. 32:2)
Shield (Ps. 33:20)
Star (Num. 24:17)
Stone (Isa. 8:14)
Stronghold (Zech. 9:12)
Sun (Mal. 4:2)
Sword (Rev. 19:15)
Vine (John 15:1)
Wall (Zech. 2:5)
Water (Rev. 22:17)
Way (John 14:6)

21
SYMBOLS OF CHRIST

```
L A V O W O D A H S D S F D G D
U I D J C R O A L U C E T O R V
R I G N O X B I B N Q G E O F I
R O H H O I O M E G A B W R N N
S T C A T N U L Y I H S M E W E
Z N J K L W Q A P A T L L A W O
A K R M Y K S B L V W M P X L P
S A N C T U A R Y R A T S Y A D
P L A N T R A T S G N I N R O M
F O U N D A T I O N N G I S N E
E N O T S R E N R O C W A T E R
M O S N A R S T R O N G H O L D
S T I U R F T S R I F T I U R F
X D R N C A R K B E O B P F Q L
T B R S S D O J R O R R A Q A I
H O R E L Y O D A N A T B L O L
H I S E G R T R N M O E P P W Y
I F I D A I E L C L C H A E O N
W H E T V D J K H H A Z D G C U
S U S U T N I A T N U O F V W S
```

FORTY NEW TESTAMENT PERSONALTIES

This list of names of forty people is chosen from the Bible stories of the New Testament. Some are men; some are women. Can you find their names in the puzzle?

Agrippa	Jesus	Nathaniel
Ananias	John	Paul
Andrew	Joseph	Peter
Bartholomew	Judas	Philip
Caesar	Jude	Rhoda
Demas	Justus	Silas
Dorcas	Lazarus	Simeon
Elizabeth	Lois	Stephen
Eutychus	Luke	Thomas
Felix	Lydia	Timothy
Festus	Matthew	Titus
Gamaliel	Mark	Zebedee
Jairus	Martha	
James	Mary	

22
FORTY NEW TESTAMENT PERSONALTIES

```
B  T  N  A  L  T  O  N  H  O  J  E  S  U  S  T
O  A  D  O  H  R  A  C  H  B  D  U  K  B  I  A
S  N  R  B  E  O  W  T  I  S  R  T  H  U  O  N
A  E  I  T  M  A  E  E  J  A  A  I  D  Y  L  W
D  T  E  O  H  B  N  A  Z  A  O  S  C  O  E  E
U  P  M  T  A  O  P  A  E  T  I  T  A  R  H  A
J  I  R  Z  N  P  L  D  N  F  H  R  D  M  R  F
A  A  I  B  I  P  T  O  C  I  E  N  U  O  E  U
M  L  N  R  S  N  A  R  M  E  A  Y  H  S  U  D
E  I  G  E  C  A  K  U  D  E  Q  S  T  I  A  O
S  A  S  C  H  K  M  E  L  B  W  U  R  L  W  R
E  E  D  U  J  P  B  O  T  E  S  A  E  X  N  C
U  F  S  O  T  E  E  X  H  J  I  I  I  B  U  A
T  A  U  J  Z  I  M  T  B  T  N  L  P  E  D  S
Y  H  T  O  M  I  T  O  S  A  E  P  A  V  I  E
C  R  S  S  T  A  H  E  H  F  I  L  Z  M  Y  S
H  D  U  E  M  O  B  T  G  L  S  T  E  H  A  E
U  B  J  P  A  A  A  Q  I  B  U  O  I  L  C  G
S  K  B  H  R  N  R  H  O  W  N  N  I  F  O  T
T  X  J  U  Y  B  P  K  C  A  E  S  A  R  M  A
```

JOHN THE BAPTIST: THE GREATEST PROPHET

Jesus said that "among those that are born of women there is not a greater prophet than John the Baptist" (Luke 7:28). Yet he was a very humble man and willingly took the lower place. The boldface words in this biographical sketch are hidden in the puzzle.

Mother's name was **Elisabeth** (Luke 1:5).

His father **Zacharias** could not speak until **John** was **born** (Luke 1:20).

His birth was promised by the **angel Gabriel** (Luke 1:19).

Was a **Nazarite** to the Lord (Luke 1:15).

Lived in the **deserts** (Luke 1:80).

Ate **locusts** and wild **honey** (Mark 1:6).

Was clothed with **camel's** hair and a leather **girdle** (Mark 1:6).

Began preaching near the **Jordan River** (Luke 3:3).

Told **soldiers:** "Rob no one by **violence,** be content with your **wages**" (Luke 3:14).

Told **publicans: "Collect** no more than is appointed you" (Luke 3:12).

Told the **multitude:** "He who has two **coats,** let him share with him who has **none**" (Luke 3:7-11).

People wondered if he was the **Christ** (Luke 3:15).

Proclaimed **Jesus** to be: "The **Lamb of God** who takes away the **sin** of the world" (John 1:29).

Baptized Jesus in the Jordan River (Mark 1:9-11).

Saw the Spirit of God descend on Jesus as a **dove** from **heaven** (John 1:32).

Did no **miracles** (John 10:41).

Spoke against King **Herod** (Mark 6:14-20).

Imprisoned by King Herod (Matt. 4:12).

Suffered from **doubts** (Matt. 12:2-3).

His **head** requested by the daughter of **Herodias** (Mark 6:22-25).

Beheaded in **prison** (Mark 6:27).

Buried by his **disciples** (Mark 6:29).

23
JOHN THE BAPTIST: THE GREATEST PROPHET

```
E  P  J  E  S  U  S  T  S  I  R  H  C  R  O  J
C  L  C  T  C  E  A  V  N  L  O  C  U  S  T  S
B  A  I  L  O  M  R  H  E  N  R  O  B  U  C  E
A  M  M  S  F  B  A  I  E  C  T  R  E  S  H  L
P  B  H  E  A  D  R  Y  B  S  E  G  A  W  I  C
T  O  A  G  L  B  M  F  E  P  R  I  L  M  O  A
I  F  M  O  A  S  E  V  J  O  R  D  A  N  H  R
Z  G  E  G  I  L  O  T  O  A  V  I  O  W  E  I
E  O  I  S  C  D  U  R  H  G  E  L  S  D  V  M
D  D  O  R  E  H  O  C  N  X  V  A  U  O  F  P
C  O  A  T  S  P  A  N  G  E  L  T  F  L  N  R
S  U  H  W  A  Z  P  U  B  L  I  C  A  N  S  I
E  B  T  C  E  L  L  O  C  T  E  S  W  S  E  S
L  T  G  A  N  H  S  A  L  C  R  S  A  T  L  O
P  S  N  I  F  T  K  U  N  E  H  I  I  S  W  N
I  A  S  O  R  C  M  E  I  C  D  R  H  R  E  E
C  F  P  E  Y  D  L  D  V  O  A  S  W  N  A  D
S  R  S  M  H  O  L  T  R  Z  H  C  O  L  C  W
I  E  K  T  I  O  H  E  A  V  E  N  I  H  F  U
D  A  G  V  S  W  H  N  O  C  L  R  E  V  I  R
```

24
SOLOMON'S TEMPLE

The temple built by King Solomon in Jerusalem for the worship of God was probably the most beautiful building ever built. You can read about it in I Kings 6 — 8 and II Chronicles 2 — 7. The words in this puzzle list are chosen from the story of the building of the temple.

Aaron's rod
altar
ark
basins
beams
brass
candlestick
cedar
censer
chains
chambers
chapiter
cheribim
court
fir
flowers

gold
holy place
knops
lavers
lilies
linen
lintel
lions
manna
mercy seat
molten sea
nails
nets
olive
oracle
oxen

parlors
pillar
pomegranate
porch
pots
stairs
stone
table of shewbread
treasuries
tongs
veil
wheels
windows
wings
wreaths

24
SOLOMON'S TEMPLE

```
T  C  H  A  I  N  S  T  A  E  S  Y  C  R  E  M
P  A  R  L  O  R  S  S  T  E  N  S  S  L  R  O
O  N  B  A  S  I  N  S  M  C  S  G  J  E  S  T
R  D  O  L  I  N  T  E  L  A  N  O  T  R  S  R
C  L  A  V  E  R  S  J  R  I  E  I  E  R  M  E
H  E  W  L  N  O  G  B  W  T  P  B  A  I  O  A
A  S  X  I  R  A  F  T  P  A  M  L  B  C  L  S
S  T  O  N  E  L  I  S  H  A  L  I  V  N  T  U
R  I  F  E  X  H  A  C  H  I  R  N  E  A  E  R
L  C  A  N  T  B  O  C  P  E  Y  D  I  I  N  I
I  K  N  O  P  S  W  L  H  O  W  R  L  L  S  E
O  B  N  B  L  R  D  C  Y  I  S  B  I  S  E  S
N  G  T  E  E  O  P  A  N  P  D  F  R  X  A  W
S  O  E  A  P  E  S  D  L  O  L  I  V  E  G  C
R  H  T  D  L  E  O  X  T  O  O  A  N  T  A  E
W  H  O  C  I  W  A  R  W  I  G  U  C  B  H  D
S  L  A  L  S  N  U  E  S  N  E  X  O  E  L  A
T  R  I  B  N  O  R  K  C  E  N  S  E  R  U  R
O  L  U  A  C  S  D  O  R  S  N  O  R  A  A  K
P  O  M  E  G  R  A  N  A  T  E  R  A  T  L  A
```

JONAH: DISOBEDIENT PROPHET

The best-known part of the Book of Jonah is probably the story of the storm and Jonah being swallowed by the great fish. But this Old Testament book also shows God's great love. His mercy for the people of Nineveh is clearly told in Jonah 3:10 "And God saw their works, that they turned from their evil way; and God repented of the evil he had said that he would do unto them; and he did it not." The words in the list below are important ones from the Book of Jonah. All may be found in the puzzle.

Nineveh	great fish	preached
Tarshish	swallow	forty days
	three days	overthrown
flee	three nights	
ship	prayed	sackcloth
great wind	vomited	repented
tempest		gracious
fast asleep		merciful
		spare city
shipmaster		
mariners		gourd
afraid		shadow
cast lots		angry
into the sea		worm
calm		wither

25
JONAH: DISOBEDIENT PROPHET

```
S W A L L O W H N H E V E N I N
H A C D A F S B D E H C A E R P
I O C E C I V D I D O H N H O R
P I R K H N E R N L U W A I U A
M E G S C T V I S C O B N X F Y
A B R L N L W U N R W T S A T E
S A O E C T O S H E O Y I S U D
T H P D A I T T O T A H E E L F
E E F E C O R N H D C P N A C P
R H R A L E A E E K M B C T M I
D G R T V U S E V E N O G E O H
M G S O S E R Y T I C E R A P S
T A N E A H B C A W H C U L I Y
C N R U T K C V O M I T E D R A
A G O I D E K R N F L A G E O D
L R A R N Q M O U C O I H L R Y
M Y U O G E U L B L E T I D C T
B O C F T H R E E N I G H T S R
G R E A T F I S H W O D A H S O
A F R A I D P E E L S A T S A F
```

26
UNITS OF MEASURE IN THE BIBLE

Units of measure are mentioned in both the Old and the New Testament. All of them listed in the five different categories below are found in the puzzle below. Can you find them?

Dry Measures
  Cab (II Kings 6:25)
  Ephah (Lev. 19:36)
  Homer (Num. 11:32)
  Omer (Exod. 16:36)

Measures of Length
  Cubit (Jer. 52:21)
  Fathom (Acts 27:28)
  Finger (Jer. 52:21)
  Furlong (Luke 24:13)
  Line (Jer. 31:39)
  Mile (Matt. 5:41)
  Palm (I Kings 7:26)
  Reed (Ezek. 40:5)
  Span (Exod. 28:16)

Liquid Measures
  Bath (Isa. 5:10)
  Hin (Exod. 29:40)
  Log (Lev. 14:10)

Measures of Weight
  Bekah (Exod. 38:26)
  Gerah (Num. 18:16)
  Shekel (Gen. 24:22)
  Talent (Zech. 5:7)

Roman Money
  Farthing (Matt. 10:29)
  Mite (Luke 12:59)
  Penny (Matt. 20:2)
  Pound (Luke 19:16)

26
UNITS OF MEASURE IN THE BIBLE

```
S  P  A  N  B  M  S  A  O  K  C  M  A
C  H  P  R  T  L  Q  U  H  A  R  E  G
L  O  E  S  W  A  C  E  S  L  K  N  N
U  M  L  K  O  P  M  S  P  U  I  K  O
O  E  U  B  E  U  K  C  D  H  C  M  L
B  R  A  T  A  L  E  N  T  N  A  P  R
L  T  I  S  C  B  O  R  L  T  C  H  U
S  M  K  N  L  N  A  C  O  P  N  E  F
A  O  P  A  S  F  D  T  W  I  X  D  I
T  H  O  M  E  L  I  O  H  E  L  T  Y
C  T  V  A  Q  B  T  N  S  O  H  N  K
O  A  N  D  U  K  P  E  G  Z  N  P  O
W  F  E  C  T  L  Q  C  A  E  H  T  C
T  E  N  A  D  N  U  O  P  L  R  A  S
R  O  I  B  E  K  A  H  G  I  C  H  L
M  C  L  K  O  S  B  P  T  M  B  M  A
```

NAMES OF THE HOLY SPIRIT

The third person of the Trinity is referred to by many different names, both in the Old Testament and the New Testament. Below are the names used and the Scripture passage in which they are found. The boldface words are found in the puzzle.

Spirit of **Adoption** (Rom. 8:15)

Spirit of **Burning** (Isa. 4:4)

Spirit of **Christ** (Rom. 8:9)

Spirit of **Counsel** (Isa. 11:2)

Spirit of **Faith** (II Cor. 4:13)

Spirit of the **Father** (Matt. 10:20)

Spirit of **Glory** (I Peter 4:14)

Spirit of **God** (Gen. 1:2)

Spirit of **Grace** (Heb. 10:29)

Spirit of **Holiness** (Rom. 1:4)

Spirit of **Judgment** (Isa. 4:4)

Spirit of **Knowledge** (Isa. 11:2)

Spirit of **Life** (Rom. 8:2)

Spirit of **Love** (II Tim. 1:7)

Spirit of **Might** (Isa. 11:2)

Spirit of **Promise** (Eph. 1:13)

Spirit of **Prophecy** (Rev. 19:10)

Spirit of **Revelation** (Eph. 1:17)

Spirit of **Supplication** (Zech. 12:10)

Spirit of **Truth** (John 14:17)

Spirit of **Understanding** (Isa. 11:2)

Spirit of **Wisdom** (Eph. 1:17)

27
NAMES OF THE HOLY SPIRIT

```
G  A  D  B  N  O  I  T  A  C  I  L  P  P  U  S
H  D  E  O  G  L  E  S  N  U  O  C  Z  N  O  S
D  O  G  C  T  S  I  R  H  C  O  A  D  M  V  E
R  P  R  Q  T  E  A  F  P  O  J  E  U  O  N  N
H  T  F  E  O  R  S  I  E  A  R  N  N  E  R  I
O  I  V  F  H  N  U  C  H  S  Z  O  K  Y  O  L
I  O  B  H  A  T  A  T  T  Q  I  T  J  G  S  O
L  N  C  Z  E  R  A  A  H  T  I  M  K  L  P  H
G  E  P  M  G  E  N  F  A  H  M  M  O  O  L  A
N  N  O  E  G  D  E  L  W  O  N  K  L  R  R  F
I  Q  M  Y  I  S  E  B  D  X  A  M  A  Y  P  A
N  D  I  N  T  V  C  S  Y  F  S  G  W  U  X  I
R  M  G  L  E  V  I  X  J  U  D  G  M  E  N  T
U  R  H  R  K  W  U  W  S  J  E  W  P  V  Q  H
B  D  T  I  L  S  T  Y  C  E  H  P  O  R  P  A
```

28
DAVID: A MAN AFTER GOD'S OWN HEART

David is referred to as a man who "followed me [God] with all his heart" (I Kings 14:8). As a young man he suffered much because of Saul's jealousy; yet in the end God made him king of a great nation. Although he often sinned, he always repented and confessed his sin. The boldface words in the following biographical sketch are hidden in the puzzle.

Was **born** in **Bethlehem** (I Sam. 17:12).
Son of **Jesse** (Ruth 4:17, 22).
Of the **tribe** of **Judah** (I Chron. 28:4).
Was the **youngest** of eight sons (I Sam. 16:11).
Kept his father's **sheep** (I Sam. 16:11, 13).
Played his **harp** for **King Saul** (I Sam. 16:14-23).
Killed **Goliath** (I Sam. 17:4, 54).
Was loved by **Jonathan** (I Sam. 18:1).
Fled for his **life** when Saul tried to kill him (I Sam. 19:1-18).
Lived in a **cave** (I Sam. 22:1-4).
Spared Saul's life (I Sam. 24:1-22).
Was made **king** of all **Israel** (II Sam. 5:3).
Moved the **Ark of the Lord** to **Jerusalem** (I Chron. 15:3).
Desired to build a **temple** (I Chron. 28:2).
Committed adultery with **Bathsheba** (II Sam. 11:1-5).
Confessed his sin (Ps. 51:1-19).
His son **Absalom** tried to take his **throne** (II Sam. 15:1-31).
Wept for his dead son (II Sam. 19:15-23).
Sinned in **numbering** Israel (II Sam. 24:1-14).
Bought a threshing floor on which to **worship** (II Sam. 24:18-25).
Made **preparations** to build the temple (I Chron. 22:5, 14).
Charged his son **Solomon** to do so (I Kings 2:1-9).
Was an **ancestor** of **Christ** (Matt. 1:1).
Is listed as a **hero** of **faith** (Heb. 11:32-33).

DAVID: A MAN AFTER GOD'S OWN HEART

```
H  C  A  R  C  A  V  E  O  R  E  H  A  D  U  J
A  E  H  Y  O  W  U  H  F  A  K  V  I  N  N  E
R  G  D  R  L  F  O  C  U  I  T  E  S  C  O  S
P  M  Y  G  I  C  A  R  N  G  L  K  P  Q  U  S
N  S  E  O  V  S  T  G  S  U  A  Z  T  B  T  E
U  N  W  L  U  C  T  E  A  H  L  O  P  K  D  C
M  O  C  I  V  N  O  S  M  C  I  E  E  W  L  O
B  I  D  A  L  C  G  E  O  P  E  P  W  I  A  N
E  T  O  T  F  N  L  E  A  H  L  R  W  E  D  F
R  A  N  H  I  A  O  D  S  D  I  E  P  R  P  E
I  R  O  K  S  L  I  A  H  T  N  K  O  O  G  S
N  A  D  U  N  D  K  R  M  A  D  L  B  T  L  S
G  P  R  S  P  A  R  E  D  I  E  T  H  S  A  E
A  E  T  I  M  D  H  N  A  H  V  R  N  E  T  D
J  R  D  B  G  E  I  T  T  B  O  Y  O  C  B  L
B  P  E  H  L  L  V  F  A  N  S  I  M  N  O  E
N  R  A  H  U  F  O  R  E  N  E  A  O  A  D  A
R  V  T  D  E  K  D  V  K  C  O  S  L  K  Q  R
O  E  B  I  R  T  F  A  I  T  H  J  O  O  U  S
B  U  B  A  T  H  S  H  E  B  A  W  S  B  M  I
```

MOTHERS AND SONS

Match the name of the son listed in the first column with the name of his mother found in the second column. Then find the names of both in the puzzle.

SONS	MOTHERS
1. _____ Abel	A. Rebekah
2. _____ Benjamin	B. Hagar
3. _____ Simeon	C. Leah
4. _____ Isaac	D. Jochebed
5. _____ Jacob	E. Rachel
6. _____ John the Baptist	F. Rahab
7. _____ Samuel	G. Elizabeth
8. _____ Obed	H. Bilhah
9. _____ Gershom	I. Ruth
10. _____ Moses	J. Zilpah
11. _____ Solomon	K. Asenath
12. _____ Boaz	L. Eve
13. _____ Dan	M. Eunice
14. _____ Ishmael	N. Mary
15. _____ Asher	O. Sarah
16. _____ Ahaziah	P. Zipporah
17. _____ Timothy	Q. Bathsheba
18. _____ Ephraim	R. Milcah
19. _____ James	S. Jezebel
20. _____ Laban	T. Hannah

29
MOTHERS AND SONS

```
E U N I C E N G E R S H O M T A
M S O A C O L I Z R A H A B B B
N I F D M A U M A R Y C T E V E
O W L O I L A R A H I T N S B L
J B L C E P O S T E C J E O R E
E O D I A S T O I N A D A A O A
S U H R U H M Z L M T Z G C S H
P A S N E I R H I S E A I N O G
H B L E T P A N A L H O B E D B
C E R I D H O S W T P E N R E S
R H A C L T E I E Z N A S V B A
U S L I U N C B O R K U H O E R
T H B R A Y A H A Z I A H I H K
H T V T R Z Z I P P O R A H C E
A A H Y I B K N E I T E D P O P
K B N L O R T B S N M I V C J H
E U E N I P V C Y L O K S B A R
B N A B A L E A M H S I U T M A
E T V O C H B J E Z E B E L E I
R A C H E L E U M A S H E R S M
```

OLD TESTAMENT PERSONS WHOSE NAMES BEGIN WITH THE LETTER "M"

Here are thirty-one names of persons in the Old Testament whose names begin with the letter **M**. Some of the names are familiar, but others are obscure names that increase the difficulty of the puzzle.

Maai	Micah
Mahli	Micaiah
Mahlon	Michael
Malachi	Michal
Manasseh	Miriam
Manoah	Mizzah
Maoch	Moab
Maon	Mordecai
Mattaniah	Moses
Medad	Moza
Medan	Muppim
Melcham	Mushi
Melchizedek	
Memucan	
Mephibosheth	
Merab	
Meshach	
Meshech	
Methuselah	

30
OLD TESTAMENT PERSONS WHOSE NAMES BEGIN
WITH THE LETTER "M"

```
M I C A H T E H S O B I H P E M
I B E C H B F A G O D E C I O E
P N M E D A D I H C A L A M N L
P Z O D Z M J M E I N Z Z A B C
U O R O E I I H A E L A I N M H
M O M Q C Z M C G E D M A O Y A
E S M V Z P E Y A Y L D Z A L M
M P I A U D L H F I E A K H K A
U Q H A R E C E H M A E J L Z N
C R P O T I Q C A X D H E A X A
A E M S M K O J S E S O M H X S
N E A B D A S A Z B K F G C M S
O I H F M R F I I W A T U I M E
A D L Q M A H L O N M R H M W H
M U I T R C V M Z H I S E W T C
I S T G L M O A B V U A V M A E
R H C E P A W X H M U Z A M A H
I G M A T T A N I A H I R M I S
A C P Z E N O M M B M E M P O E
M E T H U S E L A H C A H S E M
```

TWELVES

Hidden in this puzzle are persons, objects, units of measurement, etc., all of which are mentioned by twelves in the Bible.

twelve **cubits**
twelve **days**
twelve **hours**
twelve **months**
twelve **years**

twelve **bulls**
twelve **bullocks**
twelve **he-goats**
twelve **lambs**
twelve **lions**
twelve **oxen**
twelve **rams**

twelve **baskets**
twelve **bowls**
twelve **cakes**
twelve **spoons**

twelve **legions**
twelve **tribes**

twelve **gates**
twelve **foundations**
twelve **pillars**
twelve **stones**
twelve **thrones**
twelve **wells**

twelve **apostles**
twelve **brethren**
twelve **disciples**
twelve **officers**
twelve **patriarchs**
twelve **priests**
twelve **princes**
twelve **servants**
twelve **sons**

twelve **pearls**
twelve **stars**
twelve **signs**
twelve **rods**

31
TWELVES

```
T R I B E S N O O P S E N O T S
H F A Q M S N O I G E L D O I L
R B O R C D S K C O L L U B K L
O S T U V P E J G A T E S N S U
N O X E N B K B T F S C E D O B
E E T O U D X R S E O V W I A O
S L L E W S A E O R P H L S X W
T A E I A J L T W O A U K C N L
N S G S H S J H I G N E S I A S
A H M E N I A R Z O T M Y P O Y
V A S O R O L E M S N S A L D A
R G I K T U S N H K A S L E P D
E L Y S V O H C O F B A R S A R
S H T N O M R G U P M Z E A C O
E S W E D A F S R B R A O R T D
C L F X I I Q J S Y Y I S Q Z S
N S E R R E M C R A N T E U B I
I F T W P D O F F I C E R S V G
R A H E G O A T S L R A E P T N
P I L L A R S T I B U C A K E S
```

PAUL: THE GREAT MISSIONARY

Paul's conversion caused a dramatic change in his life. It continued to be an exciting life, although one of great stress at times. The boldface words in this biographical sketch are hidden in the puzzle.

Former name was **Saul** (Acts 13:9).
Was born in **Tarsus** (Acts 21:39).
Was raised to be a strict **Pharisee** (Acts 23:6).
Was a **Roman citizen** (Acts 22:25-28).
Was taught by **Gamaliel** (Acts 22:3).
Was of the tribe of **Benjamin** (Rom. 11:1).
Was a **tent maker** by trade (Acts 18:1, 3).
Persecuted the **Christians** (Acts 9:1).
Kept coats of those who stoned **Stephen** (Acts 7:58).
Met **Jesus** on the road to **Damascus** (Acts 9:4-5).
Blindness caused by bright light was healed by **Ananias** (Acts 9:11-17).
Was **baptized** (Acts 9:18).
Went to **Arabia** (Gal. 1:17).
Began his **ministry** in Damascus (Gal. 1:17-18).
Escaped in a **basket** let down over the **wall** (Acts 9:25).
Was befriended by **Barnabas** (Acts 9:27).
Was called to **preach** to the **Gentiles** (Acts 26:13-20).
Made three **missionary** journeys (Acts 13 — 26).
Suffered many things for the **gospel** (II Cor. 11:24-30).
Was taken as a **prisoner** to **Rome** (Acts 27).
Wrote many **books** of the **New Testament.**
Was probably **killed** by **Nero.**

32
PAUL: THE GREAT MISSIONARY

```
R O M E H E R F D A M A S C U S
R O E B I S N J G O S P E L U A
M J M G T U S E C T I P F S I U
I E D A B Y N F H A Y H R O W L
S I O M N T L A R V P A C A C L
S C W A I C H G I O T R D I O A
I U R L O R I H S D C I H R N W
O T E I T H C T T J E S U S E B
N S G E N A I K I L L E D G W G
A O D L E C R S A Z T E A B T D
R Y V R T N T D N H E R E H E A
Y R P O S E Z W S T D N D Z S N
V T I D P D N A I E J H I R T O
U S F H O R B T R A M T E N A S
D I E G S A I E M D P N T L M A
E N T H N K F I W A O E B I E I
G I W R A F N S B S K L N G N N
H M A N U D G O I S D E E S T A
T B W S L T H R A T H M R A D N
A I B A R A P B N D B O O K S A
```

FATHERS AND SONS

First match the names of these fathers and sons. Then find
the names of both in the puzzle.

FATHERS	SONS
1. _____ Adam	A. Abraham
2. _____ Abraham	B. Solomon
3. _____ Jesse	C. Samson
4. _____ Kish	D. Manasseh
5. _____ Terah	E. Esau
6. _____ Zebedee	F. Isaac
7. _____ Nun	G. Lot
8. _____ David	H. Abihu
9. _____ Noah	I. Rehoboam
10. _____ Joseph	J. Jeroboam
11. _____ Manoah	K. Seth
12. _____ Shaphat	L. Jonathan
13. _____ Aaron	M. Shem
14. _____ Isaac	N. Gad
15. _____ Nebat	O. David
16. _____ Solomon	P. John
17. _____ Zacharias	Q. Elisha
18. _____ Haran	R. James
19. _____ Saul	S. Joshua
20. _____ Jacob	T. Saul

33
FATHERS AND SONS

```
A  B  R  A  H  A  M  R  T  O  C  E  S  S  E  J
D  M  I  R  A  C  B  O  G  A  D  H  L  U  O  O
A  A  T  U  R  V  I  R  N  D  E  S  A  S  B  S
M  D  V  K  A  O  N  E  A  M  O  L  H  F  R  E
H  N  C  I  N  M  A  V  Z  H  B  U  I  L  J  P
L  U  A  S  D  U  I  N  O  U  A  G  T  S  O  H
A  N  H  H  C  D  L  E  S  E  P  M  E  O  H  M
R  J  A  M  E  S  A  U  I  J  A  C  T  L  U  A
E  C  R  H  A  P  R  M  O  N  V  E  R  O  K  N
I  M  E  L  U  N  S  N  O  C  I  A  L  M  H  I
S  E  T  H  Z  I  A  A  R  O  N  F  L  O  T  O
A  R  I  L  R  T  H  S  S  M  U  W  J  N  K  C
A  K  O  P  H  L  U  A  S  K  R  G  A  L  J  D
C  U  R  A  S  T  I  H  R  E  H  O  B  O  A  M
A  I  N  Z  I  R  A  N  L  G  H  I  I  H  C  N
A  L  O  T  A  P  U  S  H  M  O  T  H  L  O  O
S  M  U  H  H  R  O  A  G  H  U  S  U  C  B  S
I  Y  C  A  U  C  N  E  B  A  T  L  Y  E  H  M
K  A  T  I  J  E  R  O  B  O  A  M  T  K  R  A
Z  E  B  E  D  E  E  H  Y  N  O  M  O  L  O  S
```

TITLES OF CHRIST

Of the hundreds of titles of Christ, many are derived from social distinctions and occupations. Hidden in this puzzle are thirty-two of these titles.

Advocate (I John 2:1)
Bishop (I Peter 2:25)
Carpenter (Mark 6:3)
Comforter (John 14:16)
Counsellor (Isa. 9:6)
Daysman (Job 9:33)
Deliverer (Rom. 11:26)
Example (I Peter 2:21)
Forerunner (Heb. 6:20)
Friend (Matt. 11:19)
Guest (Luke 19:7)
Guide (Luke 1:79)
Heir (Heb. 1:2)
Intercessor (Rom. 8:34)
Interpreter (Job 33:23)
Judge (Mic. 5:1)
Keeper (John 17:12)
Leader (Isa. 55:4)
Lord (Acts 2:36)

Master (Matt. 8:19)
Nazarene (Matt. 2:23)
Physician (Matt. 9:12)
Purifier (Mal. 3:3)
Rabbi (John 1:38)
Refiner (Mal. 3:3)
Servant (Isa. 42:1)
Shepherd (John 10:11)
Sower (Matt. 13:37)
Surety (Heb. 7:22)
Teacher (John 3:2)
Testator (Heb. 9:16)
Witness (Rev. 1:5)

34
TITLES OF CHRIST

```
R  I  B  B  A  R  A  B  C  Y  H  S  I  R  J  K
E  R  E  H  C  A  E  T  T  O  E  M  E  L  N  R
Q  D  E  R  O  S  S  E  C  R  E  T  N  I  P  E
A  F  P  H  U  R  R  Q  V  S  N  T  U  V  G  T
E  G  U  B  N  U  A  A  Z  E  Y  X  W  D  P  R
L  O  R  D  S  E  N  F  P  H  R  R  U  G  H  O
G  U  I  D  E  T  L  R  K  J  E  J  I  H  Y  F
R  M  F  N  L  Q  A  R  S  W  R  I  T  R  S  M
E  P  I  O  L  C  W  W  O  V  E  U  R  E  I  O
N  X  E  Y  O  Z  I  S  K  E  V  M  R  N  C  C
I  C  R  B  R  A  T  J  D  N  I  A  E  N  I  M
F  D  G  F  H  I  N  R  L  E  L  S  P  U  A  N
E  E  E  I  N  T  E  R  P  R  E  T  E  R  N  O
R  T  S  L  R  H  S  Q  P  A  D  E  E  E  A  Z
P  T  S  U  P  V  S  W  X  Z  A  R  K  R  M  Y
M  O  G  E  F  M  E  L  E  A  D  E  R  O  S  B
M  I  H  O  U  T  A  B  D  N  E  I  R  F  Y  C
O  S  J  S  Q  G  U  X  O  V  Y  W  X  D  A  C
P  H  L  N  I  S  A  Z  E  T  A  C  O  V  D  A
Q  K  M  P  R  B  T  E  S  T  A  T  O  R  E  D
```

KINGS AND KINGDOMS

Kings and their kingdoms have played an important role in Bible history. Match the kings listed in the column on the left with the proper kingdom in the column on the right. Then find the names of both in the puzzle.

KING	KINGDOM
1. _____ David	A. Rome
2. _____ Hezekiah	B. Gath
3. _____ Hiram	C. Moab
4. _____ Achish	D. Israel
5. _____ Pharaoh	E. Assyria
6. _____ Agag	F. Judah
7. _____ Ahasuerus	G. Persia
8. _____ Og	H. Edom
9. _____ Caesar Augustus	I. Tyre
10. _____ Nebuchadnezzar	J. Syria
11. _____ Balak	K. Israel
12. _____ Ben-hadad	L. Babylon
13. _____ Chedorlaomer	M. Elam
14. _____ Darius	N. Persia
15. _____ Hadad	O. Amalekites
16. _____ Ahab	P. Bashan
17. _____ Sennacherib	Q. Egypt

35
KINGS AND KINGDOMS

```
N A H S A B S E D O M E G A G A
E T N S D A I T A N E G A L I M
B A B Y L O N S D H L S T J S A
U M A R I H T A A S E G H U R L
C N O I D E H U H N T O R D S E
H A G A T A R N I D C E H A Q K
A T E P B O E T A H U I T H U I
D A Y S K U S P O S N W E R Y T
N G I M A I E C A I S R A E L E
E V R T L R O H B Z E Y O K T S
Z A C I S G A N E M P E R S I A
Z U H I E R H U O Z O S T I R E
A P A S U T O A G C E D I V A D
R I N C A S L E I U T K E O C A
O G H I H R N U V D S U I R A D
M A L E O I E Z O N C T E A C A
E O T D R E S B A L A K U C H H
P C E Q U I N H C L E A R S I N
P H A R A O H A K T D O M G L E
C U N E M S E N N A C H E R I B
```

SYMBOLISM IN THE BOOK OF REVELATION

Revelation, the last book of the Bible, is filled with imagery and symbolism. Hidden in this puzzle are a variety of terms used in the book, many of which are symbolic.

altar	foundations	robes
angels	fountains	seas
beasts	gates	seals
blood	girdles	smoke
books	holy city	stars
bottomless pit	horns	sun
bride	horses	thunders
candlesticks	kings	thrones
clouds	Lamb	trees
crowns	lamps	vials
dragons	minerals	virgins
earthquakes	moons	voices
elders	plagues	wings
fires	rainbow	
firstfruits	rivers	

36

SYMBOLISM IN THE BOOK OF REVELATION

```
A R O F I R S T F R U I T S T R
S N I G R I V Q E S W L V K A S
A C N P L A G U E S R I D I M A
O V R S E T A G R B A E N S N E
S O B O I A B E S L O B V G H A
N I F J W O D M S R O O E I S R
O C P N V N B C A W A L K G R T
I E U Z U N S O T L S T B S U H
T S A H G I R D L E S L S N F Q
A D T I P S S E L M O T T O B U
D U H S A N T M R O U V U G S A
N O R A S R R X D A S N S A T K
U L O E H O L Y C I T Y P R S E
O C N S B H I E L A S L M D A S
F S E E Y S E R I F L Y A W E E
S R S S M W C N X D A K L D B S
E E J R M O S L A R E N I M I R
E D O E K O O G Z O S R H N P O
R L Q F S S K N P D B E T N G H
T E C A N D L E S T I C K S O S
```

JACOB: THE CRAFTY ONE

Jacob lived a difficult life, and many times the difficulties were results of his own actions. Yet God overruled everything to bring about the good of His people, the descendants of Jacob. The boldface words in the following biographical sketch are hidden in the puzzle. All of the Scripture references are found in Genesis except the last one.

Was the grandson of **Abraham** (25:19).
Was the son of **Isaac** and Rebekah (25:20-26).
Had a **twin** brother, **Esau** (25:24-25).
Esau was a **hunter,** but Jacob was a **quiet man** who lived in tents (25:27).
Jacob bought the **birthright** from Esau for some **food** (25:30-34).
Rebekah helped Jacob **trick** his father Isaac (27:5-15).
Stole the **blessing** (27:26-33).
Feared Esau and fled to **Haran** (27:41-45).
Had a vision of the **ladder** at **Bethel** (28:12-17).
Met his Uncle **Laban** (29:13-14).
Worked **seven** years for each of his two wives, **Leah** and **Rachel** (29:15-30).
Served Laban for **cattle** (30:31-43).
Returned to **Canaan** (31:17-55).
Wrestled with an **angel** at **Peniel** (32:24-31).
Name was changed to **Israel** (32:28).
Was **reconciled** with his brother Esau (33:1-16).
Built an **altar** at Bethel (35:1-3).
Had special love for **Joseph;** made him a special **coat** (37:3).
Grieved when Joseph was thought to be dead (37:28-36).
Went to **Egypt** when Joseph was found to be **alive** (46:1-3).
Appeared before **Pharaoh** (47:7).
Blessed his sons before he died (chap. 49).
Was **buried** in the land of Canaan (50:12-13).
Is listed as a **"hero of faith"** (Heb. 11:21).

JACOB: THE CRAFTY ONE

```
I A C B H F T W I N A J L C O E
S Z O U E I R A N F O O D R S U
A E B R S H I P Y S Y R H A C A
A S V I A X C T E H G I U S A L
C E D E L C K P S L A H N Y N T
R A L D N O H V N V R G T N A A
E E V I L A P E S A D E E S A R
B C A E R N L T L E N H R A N D
E L G A E Y A R L T T P H T E R
K N O T U L R I S I B L A V S B
A H U P E O C J A T G O E C L I
H S T A E N L F H A C I R E U N
G E R P O N F G I S R U S Y A O
N S A C W O I L A G N S O M T M
I T E C O R H E C H E R T D L A
S R U R H S U N L D E E E B I H
S D E T L A N A G D I U G O N A
E H R K C M R B D U A H Y D U R
L I O A D Y O A Q T S M P S I B
B E T H E L L L N E L T T A C A
```

38
TENS

Hidden in this puzzle are animals, persons, units of measurement, etc., all of which are mentioned by tens in the Bible.

ten asses
ten bulls
ten bullocks
ten camels
ten foals
ten oxen

ten acres
ten baths
ten cubits
ten homers
ten measures
ten years

ten pounds
ten shekels
ten talents

ten tribes
ten cities

ten commandments

ten chariots

ten loaves
ten cheeses

ten candlesticks
ten curtains
ten knops
ten lavers
ten pillars
ten sockets

ten brethren
ten concubines
ten elders
ten lepers
ten princes
ten sons
ten virgins
ten women

ten horns

ten strings

38
TENS

```
S  N  I  G  R  I  V  S  T  R  I  N  G  S  L  C
R  E  A  I  K  S  N  O  K  P  A  T  U  V  A  U
E  B  N  J  T  M  R  S  Q  C  S  L  W  N  V  R
P  C  H  I  L  R  T  A  R  R  O  Y  D  X  E  T
E  D  B  F  B  N  I  E  E  A  B  L  A  Z  R  A
L  U  E  G  E  U  S  B  V  Y  E  D  L  C  S  I
C  P  Q  L  P  S  C  E  E  S  H  G  E  U  F  N
S  R  A  O  P  R  S  N  T  S  E  S  S  A  B  S
R  T  N  O  S  M  I  I  O  L  L  I  J  K  R
E  S  N  N  T  T  C  N  U  C  V  E  E  W  X  E
M  K  R  D  E  K  N  Z  C  Y  A  T  K  B  C  D
O  O  F  S  S  O  X  E  N  E  H  P  Q  E  R  L
H  F  G  S  T  I  J  M  M  R  S  S  O  S  H  E
H  O  S  K  R  O  E  N  E  D  V  H  N  U  T  S
P  A  W  E  D  A  I  N  L  M  N  T  R  O  L  S
O  L  B  C  S  J  L  R  K  O  S  A  V  E  S  E
U  S  X  U  E  E  I  L  A  P  T  B  M  X  A  I
N  Y  R  B  L  F  E  L  I  H  U  A  Z  M  B  T
D  E  Z  A  G  L  H  H  N  P  C  V  C  W  O  I
S  O  C  K  E  T  S  M  C  Q  N  E  M  O  W  C
```

NEW THINGS

The adjective **new** is applied to many things in the Bible. Thirty-three of these are hidden in this puzzle.

new **bottles** (Job 32:19)

new **cart** (I Sam. 6:7)

new **cloth** (Matt. 9:16)

new **commandment** (John 13:34)

new **cords** (Judg. 15:13)

new **court** (II Chron. 20:5)

new **covenant** (Heb. 8:8)

new **creature** (II Cor. 5:17)

new **doctrine** (Mark 1:27)

new **earth** (Isa. 65:17)

new **fruit** (Ezek. 47:12)

new **garment** (I Kings 11:29)

new **gate** (Jer. 26:10)

new **gods** (Deut. 32:17)

new **heavens** (Isa. 65:17)

new **heart** (Ezek. 36:26)

new **house** (Deut. 20:5)

new **king** (Exod. 1:8)

new **lump** (I Cor. 5:7)

new **meat offering** **(Num. 28:26)**

new **men** (Eph. 2:15)

new **mercies** (Lam. 3:23)

new **name** (Rev. 2:17)

new **sepulchre** (John 19:41)

new **song** (Ps. 40:3)

new **spirit** (Ezek. 11:19)

new **sword** (II Sam. 21:16)

new **testament** (Matt. 26:28)

new **tomb** (Matt. 27:60)

new **tongues** (Mark 16:17)

new **way** (Heb. 10:20)

new **wife** (Deut. 24:5)

new **wine** (Mark 2:22)

NEW THINGS

```
U C M T I U R F T R B O P R S G
T V O S N T U E C P W M B Y C A
A P S R I E D A S T U T C A R T
W R E R D Q M W N L R O D W R E
S A I C H S C A G O M A X O X Q
J P R I R D N Y T M E V E E T H
S B I Q H E V S A S W K N H S O
I T G A V S A N F U E I I A G U
A R X O H Y D T H G R T Q N T S
B U C U M M T E U T A G I S G E
G O D S E E A F C R F R H A R N
P C O N Z V G O E M E O M H Y A
A K T J E H D I L F T C C E M L
O W I N E D T U F A R L H I N S
G Z S O N A M O L E U O J W E T
M N W L A K T K N P N T D I B O
O G O N M A E Y E G L H C F A M
T F R S E E J S D B U R A E C B
N X D M E D N C K O E E A R T H
B O T T L E S B E M T O S I R P
```

RUTH: THE MOABITESS

Ruth 1:16 is probably the most familiar verse in the book: "And Ruth said, Entreat me not to leave thee, or to return from following after thee; for whither thou goest I will go; and where thou lodgest, I will lodge; thy people shall be my people, and thy God, my God." It is typical of the book which shows Ruth's love for her mother-in-law and God's care for them both. The hidden words in this puzzle are taken from the Book of Ruth.

Moab	Elimelech	Naomi
Judah	Mahlon	Orpah
Bethlehem	Chilion	daughters-in-law
	Boaz	Mara
	Obed	Moabitess

kinsman	barley harvest
handmaid	reapers
elders of the city	gleaned
inheritance	ephah
	winnow
	threshing floor

RUTH: THE MOABITESS

```
B A O M A R A B D E J C Z A O B
E A F P I K S N C H I L I O N E
M H R G T N O L H A M Q P W G T
Y O U L J X A Y F R O V A D I H
T B A M E S K O Z U A L Y N C L
I Z D B X Y W X C P N Z H F R E
C L N R I O H M Q I T E X O A H
E G P J N T L A S D R Z O D I E
H A C N K U E R R I B L S U K M
T E I S F N E S T V F R H A T F
F W O J M T Z A S G E C O B E D
O R P A H L N V N X L S P J L N
S I E G Z C T I D U I H T M S H
R H U X E X H Y N A M S N I K A
E A F C R S O J P S E D L Q B N
D T K W E N X R B G L E A N E D
L D Q R X A E H I N E I O T H M
E P H A H V K T D U C R F K L A
C T O G J L M Q S N H A D U J I
A I B F R E A P E R S G A R C D
```

THE TRIUNE GOD

The three persons of the Trinity are active in many ways. The names below, each indicative of a special attribute of God, are hidden in the puzzle:

Benefactor (Ps. 68:19)

Bestower (Isa. 63:7)

Commander (Isa. 55:4)

Creator (Gen. 1:1)

Counsellor (Isa. 9:6)

Deliverer (Rom. 11:26)

Father (Isa. 9:6)

Giver (I Tim. 6:17)

Governor (Matt. 2:6)

Intercessor (Isa. 53:12)

Keeper (Ps. 121:5)

Lover (I John 4:9)

Maker (Ps. 95:6)

Mediator (I Tim. 2:5)

Messenger (Mal. 3:1)

Preserver (Ps. 37:28)

Provider (Gen. 22:8)

Purposer (Eph. 3:11)

Redeemer (Job 19:25)

Restorer (Ruth 4:15)

Revealer (Dan. 2:22)

Ruler (Mic. 5:2)

Saviour (Luke 2:11)

Sustainer (Ps. 3:5)

THE TRIUNE GOD

```
R E I N T E R C E S S O R E F R
E S S I U R E V R E S E R P A E
D U G Q U B O K E C H G R U J H
N S O T L I M T V O I E Y R Z T
A T V N A M U X A N R T I P R A
M A E L O V E R W E Y O D O E F
M I R V R P L U V A R A T S M A
O N N U H O W I O X B C J E E P
C E O R A K L R Q K A C Z R E E
A R R U S E E L U F G L I R D G
E B Q O D D S I E V K E E P E R
P C F I I G C N R S I G M O R R
D E T V G T E I P O N O Y N E R
F H O A I B R U L E R U E W F E
P R J S U L P H S I X V O X C V
P U V J K I O S M W O T A C R E
R E S T O R E R O F S B W B E A
Q T R S U M N D G E M A K E R L
A U Z I B A Y E B D C D A T A E
R O T A I D E M C O D G I V E R
```

THE SHEPHERD'S PSALM

Psalm 23 is one of the best-known psalms in the Bible. It is sometime known as the Shepherd's Psalm because it speaks of God's tender care for his people. All of the boldface words are hidden in the puzzle.

1. The **Lord** is my **shepherd,** I shall not **want.**
2. He **maketh** me to **lie** down in green **pastures:** he **leadeth** me **beside** the still **waters.**
3. He **restoreth** my **soul:** he **leadeth** me in the **paths** of **righteousness** for his name's **sake.**
4. **Yea,** though I **walk** through the **valley** of the **shadow** of **death,** I will **fear** no **evil:** for **thou** art with **me;** thy **rod** and thy **staff** they **comfort me.**
5. Thou **preparest** a **table** before me in the **presence** of mine **enemies:** thou **anointest** my **head** with **oil:** my **cup runneth** over.
6. Surely **goodness** and **mercy** shall **follow** me all the **days** of my **life:** and I will **dwell** in the **house** of the **Lord** for **ever.**

42
THE SHEPHERD'S PSALM

```
Y  E  L  B  A  T  B  S  R  E  T  A  W  M  C  Y
E  D  I  R  O  D  S  E  L  C  W  R  A  E  F  H
A  G  V  T  P  E  Q  U  T  B  I  D  N  J  G  C
L  J  E  O  N  A  E  K  A  S  H  L  T  H  O  U
B  I  L  D  C  T  M  W  F  H  L  O  R  X  R  P
C  A  O  X  I  H  A  G  S  E  B  I  D  E  T  F
T  O  T  A  O  S  S  I  W  P  G  D  V  D  F  O
G  N  M  U  I  H  E  D  A  H  T  E  D  A  E  L
E  B  S  F  T  A  L  B  T  E  J  H  T  Y  W  E
C  E  B  A  O  H  K  E  C  R  X  S  B  S  M  A
N  L  P  C  X  R  O  B  I  D  R  O  L  I  E  D
E  H  C  A  F  U  T  U  X  Q  U  N  B  A  R  E
S  F  J  T  S  S  E  I  M  E  N  E  F  R  C  T
E  C  I  N  U  T  K  A  C  U  N  V  O  P  Y  H
R  A  E  L  C  G  U  X  O  Y  E  L  L  A  V  H
P  S  U  B  X  L  O  R  D  R  T  O  L  R  C  T
S  H  A  D  O  W  C  B  E  I  H  U  O  D  Z  E
O  J  A  N  O  I  N  T  E  S  T  K  W  A  L  K
U  T  S  E  R  A  P  E  R  P  L  S  A  E  G  A
L  H  T  E  R  O  T  S  E  R  F  H  W  H  E  M
```

NEHEMIAH: THE BUILDER

The Book of Nehemiah tells about the way the prophet led many Jews from the land of captivity back to Jerusalem. There they rebuilt the temple and the walls of the city. Even more importantly, they reestablished the worship of God. Can you find these key words from the Book of Nehemiah in the puzzle?

Shushan	Artaxerxes	law
Jerusalem	Asaph	usury
	Sanballat	redeemed
captivity	Tobiah	restore
cup-bearer	Geshem	rebel
sad countenance		remember
letter	Jews	
	Levites	
broken wall		
burned	arise	
mocked	build	
fox	watch	
	breaches	
	sword	
	one hand	
	trumpet	
	fortified	

43
NEHEMIAH: THE BUILDER

```
S A N B A L L A T P M E H S E G
H A X Z H A R T G W A R S W E J
U O D P W Q H E K H S H D A C E
S S A C J R F P M O L E T T E R
H S U Z O I T M S E I R B C V U
A W N R V U E U Y F M J X H K S
N O E P Y Y N R I Z B B N Q O A
D R B Z T F H T C R D F E Z B L
Z D S R A J R Q E G Z Y H R L E
H P E H X O P A S N T S K A I M
A Y X O F L C H U I A Q W E U O
I L R V C H A R V L M N Y O X C
D X E T E I I I X T E A C N P K
E C X S B N T S H K Z K A E Y E
M F A O K P T U O Z J B Q H S D
E P T V A B G R V A X L T A R O
E O R C U P B E A R E R U N E G
D G A P Q K S B U I L D C D B F
E J K C L H O D N S B U R N E D
R E S T O R E F S E T I V E L A
```

1
CHRISTIAN VIRTUES

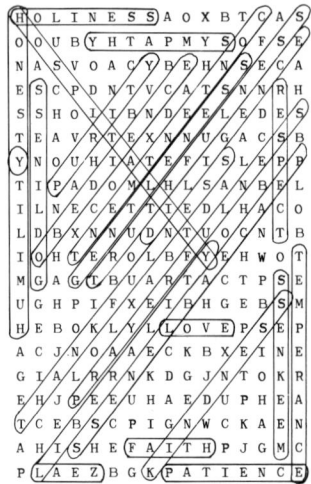

2
NAMES FOR CHRISTIANS

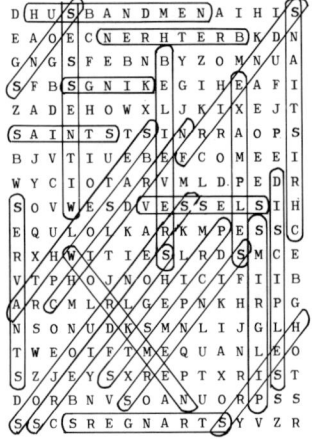

3
THE WORK OF THE HOLY SPIRIT

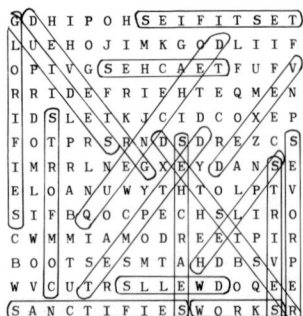

4
DANIEL: THE BRAVE ONE

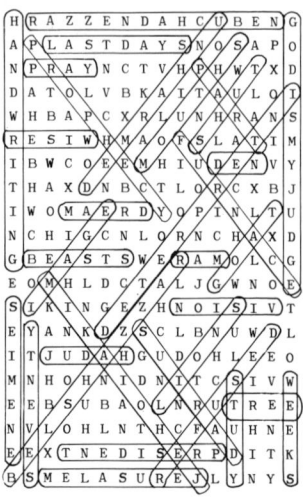

5
DREAMS AND DREAMERS

MATCHING: 1-C, 2-I, 3-F, 4-J, 5-H, 6-A, 7-K, 8-L, 9-E, 10-G, 11-B, 12-D

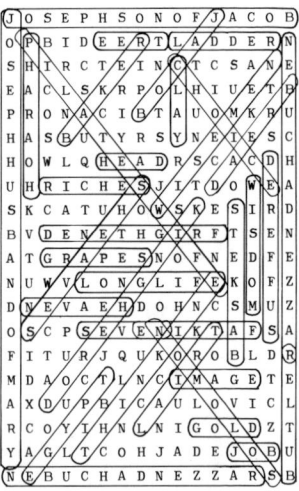

6
THE HEBREW ALPHABET

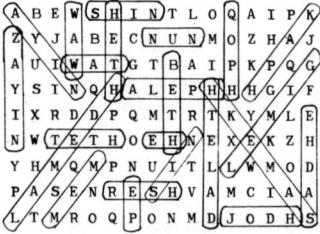

7
THE GREEK ALPHABET

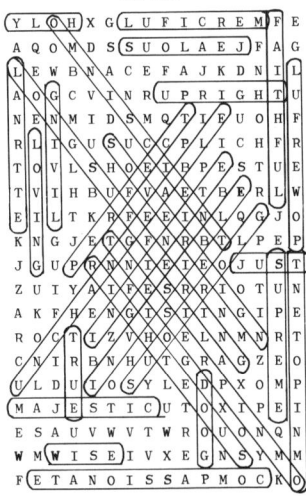

8
GOD IS...

9
OLD TESTAMENT NAMES THAT BEGIN WITH "A"

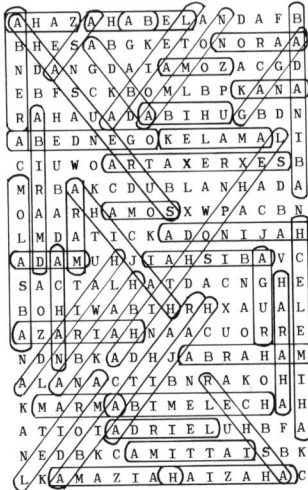

10
HOLY THINGS

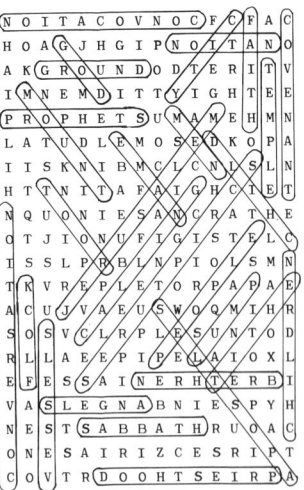

11
ANOINTINGS

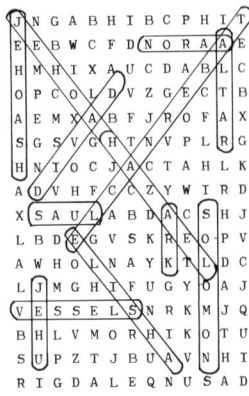

12
SAMSON: THE WEAK STRONG MAN

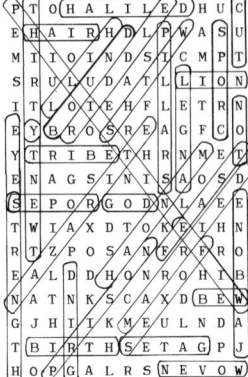

13
"LORD, LORD"

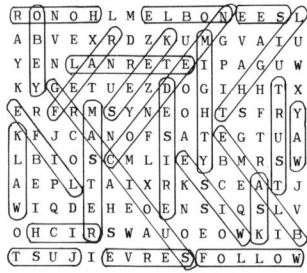

14
FORTY OLD TESTAMENT PERSONALITIES

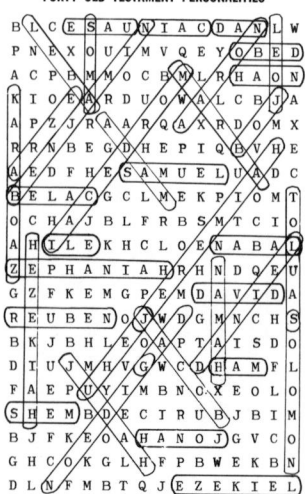

15
AMOS: SHEPHERD FROM TEKOA

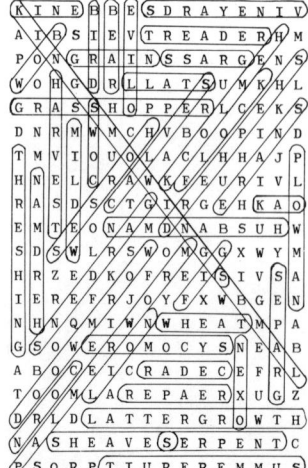

16
MOSES: THE LEADER

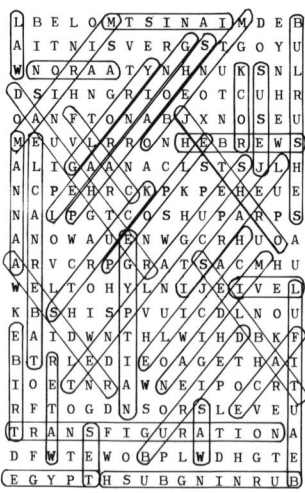

17
"FEAR NOT"

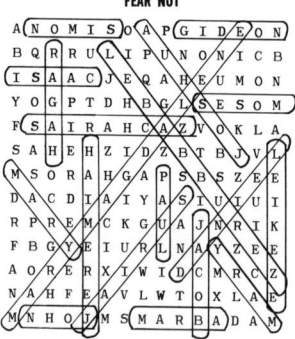

18
CITIES AND SITES (1)

MATCHING: 1-D, 2-E, 3-I, 4-M, 5-W, 6-K, 7-X, 8-A, 9-G, 10-S, 11-U, 12-L, 13-V, 14-H, 15-T, 16-F, 17-B, 18-J, 19-N, 20-C, 21-O, 22-P, 23-R, 24-Q

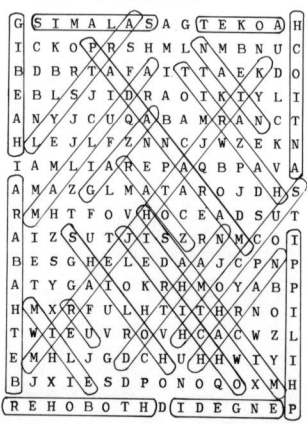

19
CITIES AND SITES (2)

MATCHING: 1-N, 2-R, 3-M, 4-S, 5-V, 6-A, 7-H, 8-X, 9-T, 10-O, 11-B, 12-G, 13-P, 14-L, 15-I, 16-J, 17-K, 18-Q, 19-F, 20-D, 21-E, 22-U, 23-W, 24-C

20
CITIES AND SITES (3)

MATCHING: 1-I, 2-X, 3-R, 4-O, 5-G, 6-B, 7-E, 8-K, 9-N, 10-H, 11-D, 12-A, 13-W, 14-U, 15-S, 16-M, 17-T, 18-V, 19-Q, 20-P, 21-J, 22-L, 23-C, 24-F

21
SYMBOLS OF CHRIST

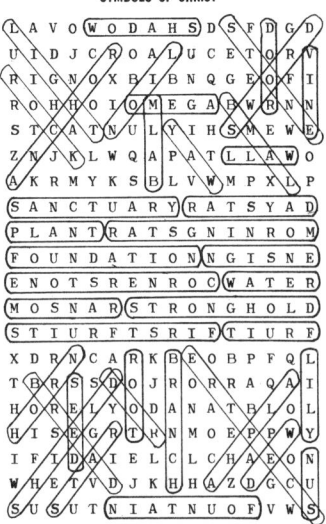

22
FORTY NEW TESTAMENT PERSONALTIES

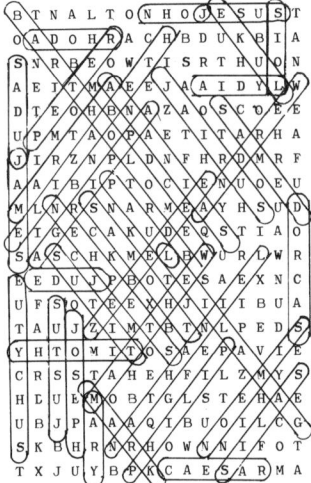

23
JOHN THE BAPTIST: THE GREATEST PROPHET

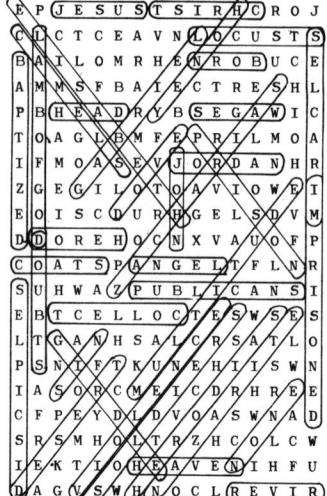

24
SOLOMON'S TEMPLE

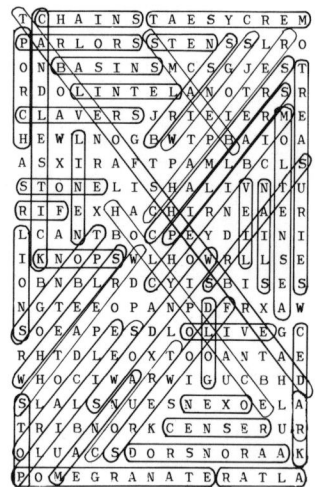

25
JONAH: DISOBEDIENT PROPHET

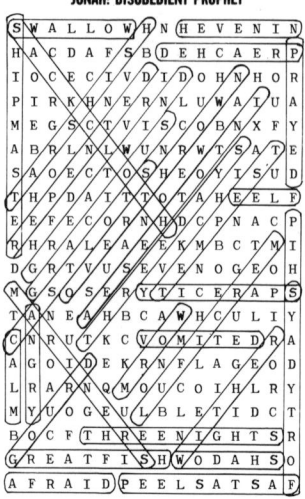

26
UNITS OF MEASURE IN THE BIBLE

27
NAMES OF THE HOLY SPIRIT

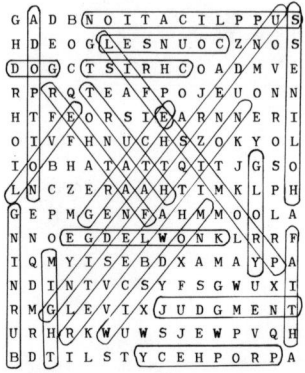

28
DAVID: A MAN AFTER GOD'S OWN HEART

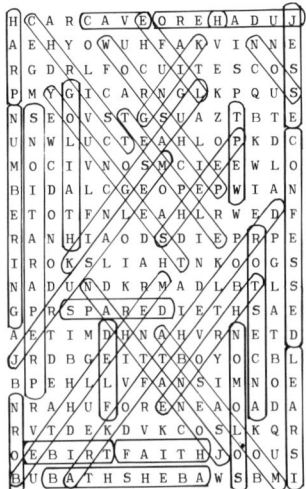

30
OLD TESTAMENT PERSONS WHOSE NAMES BEGIN WITH THE LETTER "M"

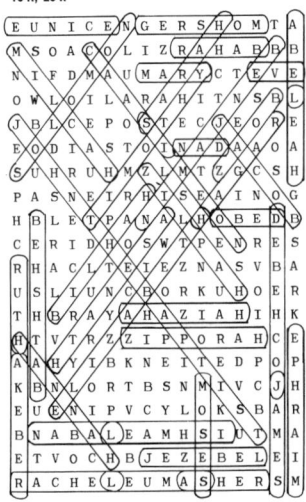

29
MOTHERS AND SONS

MATCHING: 1-L, 2-E, 3-C, 4-O, 5-A, 6-G, 7-T, 8-I, 9-P, 10-D, 11-Q, 12-F, 13-H, 14-B, 15-J, 16-S, 17-M, 18-K, 19-N, 20-R

31
TWELVES

32
PAUL: THE GREAT MISSIONARY

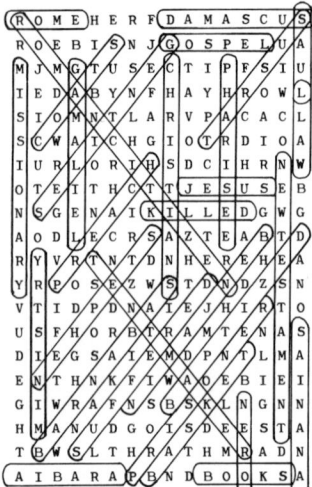

34
TITLES OF CHRIST

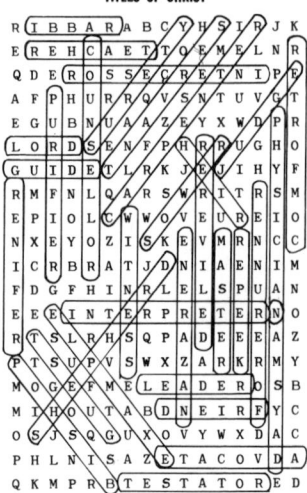

33
FATHERS AND SONS

MATCHING: 1-K, 2-F, 3-O, 4-T, 5-A, 6-R, 7-S, 8-B, 9-M, 10-D, 11-C, 12-Q, 13-H, 14-E, 15-J, 16-I, 17-P, 18-G, 19-L, 20-N

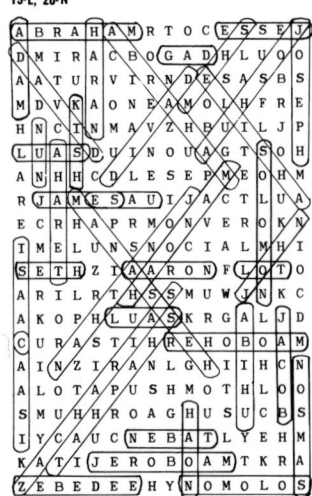

35
KINGS AND KINGDOMS

MATCHING: 1-D, 2-F, 3-I, 4-B, 5-Q, 6-O, 7-G, 8-P, 9-A, 10-L, 11-C, 12-J, 13-M, 14-N, 15-H, 16-K, 17-E

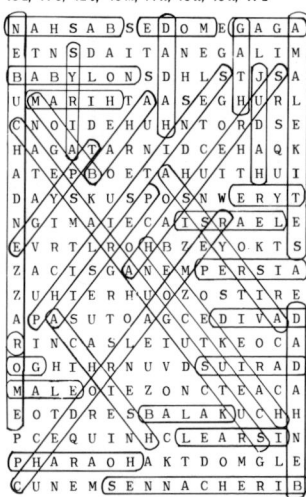

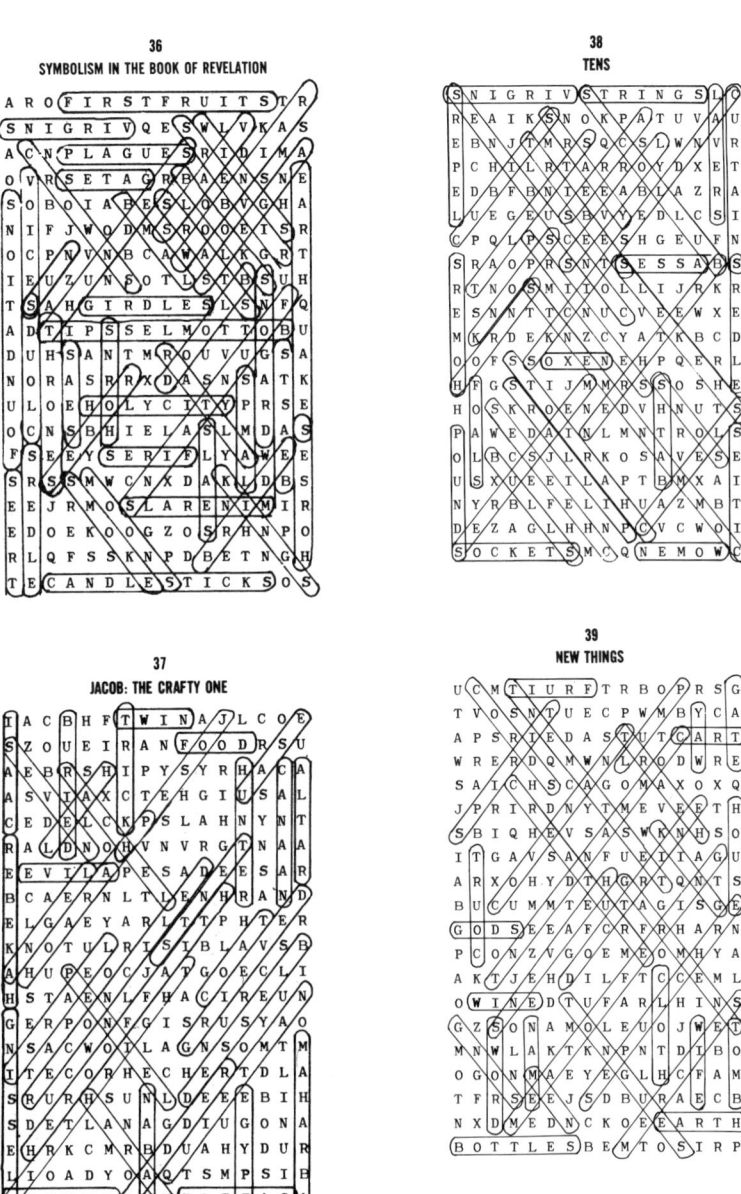

36
SYMBOLISM IN THE BOOK OF REVELATION

38
TENS

37
JACOB: THE CRAFTY ONE

39
NEW THINGS

40
RUTH: THE MOABITESS

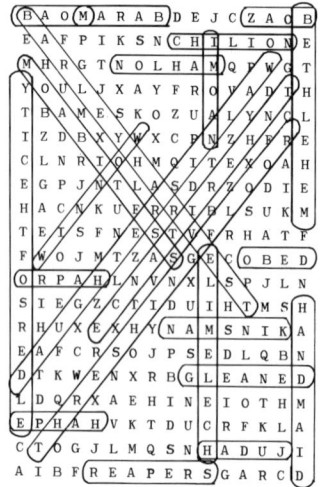

42
THE SHEPHERD'S PSALM

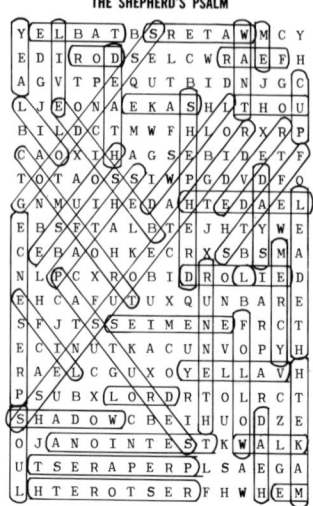

41
THE TRIUNE GOD

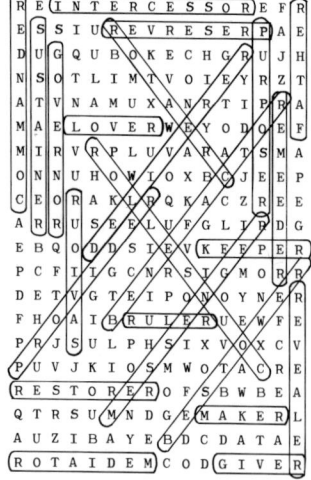

43
NEHEMIAH: THE BUILDER

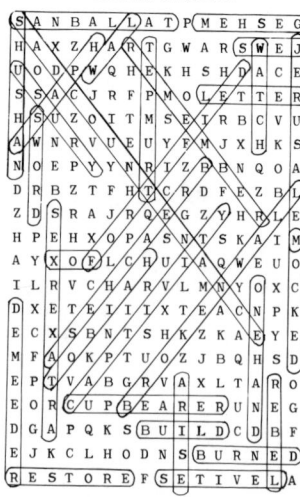